PRAISE FOR *FRANCHISE BIBLE*

Franchise Bible is the most comprehensive, step by step, go to guide for all things franchising. The best franchise book, bar none.

—Nick-Anthony Zamucen, Founder of Bio-One Inc.

Franchise Bible is the roadmap that leads to franchising success. Now in its 8th edition, *Franchise Bible* has been the go-to franchising resource for decades. Rick Grossmann and Michael Katz have more than a half-century of franchise experience between them. The expertise that each brings to the industry is a huge win for anyone reading *Franchise Bible*. To your success!

—Carolyn Miller, Founder of the National Franchise Institute

If you could earn a degree in Franchising, this would be the textbook. Whether you are considering franchising as your expansion option, or managing a mature franchise system, *Franchise Bible* is the most organized, well communicated franchise tool available. If you are serious about franchising, start here, and keep this book handy as you work through each stage of development; referencing each new section a second time as you progress. It will change the decisions you make and greatly reduce your upfront investment, while increasing your probability of success in the shortest amount of time.

—Chris Burrei, President of Franchise Development of GMXR Inc.

The resources in *Franchise Bible* are extremely valuable to us as franchise owners. When combined with our proven franchise system and leadership we are armed with all of the best tools for success.

—Gregg and Cheryl Chiasson, Instant Imprints South MetroFranchise Owners

Franchise Bible has saved our company valuable time and thousands of dollars! The strategies in this book are a must for anyone entering the franchise world.

—Dr. Kent Lauson, Founder of NEO Orthodontics Franchising

Anyone considering buying a franchise or franchising their business should start with the *Franchise Bible*. This easy to use reference guide will highlight the legal, financial, and structural details to consider before taking that important first step. Already a franchisee or franchisor? Solidify your strategy with this guide. Rick Grossmann and Michael Katz generously share their expertise in such a relatable manner that everyone can find value in its content. This guide is a must for your business reference library.

—Tricia Petteys, Executive VP Operations of Payroll Vault Franchise

Franchise Bible is the single, best source of information, whether you're considering buying a franchise or building a franchise organization. The depth of experience that Rick Grossmann and Michael Katz provide the reader is concise, organized, and thorough. Look no further than this comprehensive and easy to read guide."

—Doug Root, CEO of JungleQuest, Inc. Franchising

The culture your organization needs to become a successful franchise starts at the top, and this book helps guide you down the right decision path to be creative within best practices Rick and Michael have established. In the *Franchise Bible* they stress originality; build and buy into something that is original and creates value. In our swim school business we created something that was never done before and could be duplicated; we also realized the need for every person to be able to swim. *Franchise Bible* helps me focus on our needs as a franchisor and reawakens me to the needs of the franchisee.

—Michael Mann, President of SwimLabs

Having consulted on and developed multiple franchise units for over 10 years, we can honestly say the practical advice in the *Franchise Bible* provides a clear and comprehensive perspective of the multiple aspects of franchising that one needs to be a successful franchise owner. Wish we had this when we started!

—Erik and Wendy Skaalerud, Colorado Area Developers and Franchise Owners of Orangetheory Fitness, Capital Lending Solutions Principals

FRANCHISE BIBLE

How to **Buy a Franchise** or **Franchise Your Own Business**

EIGHTH EDITION

Rick Grossmann with **Michael J. Katz Esq.**

Entrepreneur Press, Publisher
Cover Design: Ponderosa Pine Design
Production and Composition: Ponderosa Pine Design

This publication is designed to provide accurate and authoritative information in
regard to the subject matter covered. It is sold with the understanding that the publisher is not engaged in rendering legal, accounting or other professional services. If
legal advice or other expert assistance is required, the services of a competent professional person should be sought.

Library of Congress Cataloging-in-Publication Data
Names: Grossmann, Rick, author. | Keup, Erwin J. Franchise bible.
Title: Franchise bible : how to buy a franchise or franchise your own
business / by Rick Grossmann with Michael J. Katz Esq.
Description: Eighth Edition. | Irvine, California : Entrepreneur Press, 2017.
| Revised edition of Franchise bible, c2012.
Identifiers: LCCN 2016040451| ISBN 9781599186009 (paperback) | ISBN
1599186004 (paperback)
Subjects: LCSH: Franchises (Retail trade)—United States. | Franchises
(Retail trade)—United States—Forms. | Franchises (Retail trade)—Law and
legislatio—United States.
Classification: LCC HF5429.235.U5 G766 2017 | DDC 658.8/708—dc23
LC record available at https://lccn.loc.gov/2016019781

Printed in the United States of America

21 20 19 18 17   10 9 8 7 6 5 4 3 2 1

Franchise Bible, Eighth Edition, is dedicated to our U.S. military veterans and their families that protect and sacrifice for our national freedom and enable us to build businesses and create jobs across our great nation.

Thank you for your service! www.vetstarter.com

Contents

PART I: Buying and Operating a Franchise (Becoming a Franchise Owner)

PART II: Franchise Your Business (Becoming a Franchisor)

PART III: Franchise Ten Commandments— Thou Shalt Thrive!

Foreword

For many aspiring entrepreneurs, finding a path to business ownership can be challenging. With so many great ideas, products, and services already in the market, it can be hard to think of a new niche to pursue. And if even if you do know what type of business you'd like to start, there are numerous obstacles that prevent many people from ever actually taking the leap from entrepreneurial dream to business ownership reality.

For those who have taken that leap, and have created a successful business, finding a way to expand that business can prove equally daunting. If you try to go it alone, your growth will likely be restrained by limited finances, time, energy, and resources.

These may seem like two very different problems, but whichever one you find yourself relating to, the answer to both lies in a word: franchising. The beauty of franchising is that it offers two unique and useful paths to growing a business, whether you are just starting out or you want to expand an existing business. For the aspiring entrepreneur, becoming a franchisee allows you to buy into a company that already has a proven model for success. For the existing business owner, becoming a franchisor offers a systematic way to allow others to help grow your business and brand with reduced financial risk on your part.

We at Entrepreneur pride ourselves on our coverage of the franchise industry, including the first, best, and most comprehensive franchise ranking in the world, the Franchise 500°. Over the 37-plus years we've published that ranking, we've seen how franchising has evolved and adapted to changes in the economy, business climate, and technology. Through it all, the industry continues to thrive. Franchising has made entrepreneurship possible for thousands of people who might not otherwise have ever started their own business, and helped others take their business from local success to nationally-known brand. We've talked to these people. We've listened to their success stories—as well as their struggles—and shared them often in the pages of our magazine and on our website. We've heard over and over about the positive impact that franchising has had not only on their lives and livelihoods, but on communities and economies around the country and around the world.

In short, we believe in the power of franchising.

But we also know that putting that power into action requires knowledge. That is why Entrepreneur is joining forces with franchise expert Rick Grossmann and franchise attorney Michael Katz, Esq. to bring you the eighth edition of *Entrepreneur Magazine's Franchise Bible*. Following in the footsteps of his mentor and original author of the *Franchise Bible*, Erwin Keup, Rick (along with Michael) has put together the most up-to-date, all-inclusive information on today's franchise market for both franchisees and franchisors. The *Franchise Bible* is designed as just that—a bible (no, not that one), a full-on reference for all things franchise. The book you are holding offers up easily accessible information on everything you need to get started on the franchise journey and includes value-added content both on the Entrepreneur Franchise site (www.entrepreneur.com/franchiseresources) and on the author's dedicated landing page, www.franchisebiblestudy.com. There, you will find links to useful forms and resources to help you make your franchise dreams a reality.

This updated edition includes an interactive roadmap that allows you to customize what you read and access based on your individual business circumstances and goals. It also brings you the latest information with tutorials, tips and tricks, and anecdotes and stories from franchise experts.

Whichever path you're hoping to follow—that of franchisee or franchisor—we wish you success on your entrepreneurial journey, and we're sure you'll find the *Franchise Bible* to be an invaluable guide along the way.

—Tracy Stapp Herold, Special Projects and Franchise 500® Editor

A Lifetime of Achievement

REMEMBERING ERWIN (ERV) KEUP, *FRANCHISE BIBLE* FOUNDING AUTHOR, BY RICK GROSSMANN

When I was in college I owned a small service business. I wanted to grow my business and was evaluating the different methods of expansion when I was introduced to franchising in one of my classes. I immediately fell in love with the model and started researching the options to franchise an existing business. At that time, being a young college student, resources were tight and the options were few.

I contacted numerous franchise development companies, consultants, and attorneys only to find out that the process was complicated and the investment was way beyond anything I could ever come up with. One day I went into a bookstore and was searching in the business section for books on franchising when I came across *Franchise Bible*. The author was, of course, Erwin ("Erv") J. Keup. I read the book in one day and started putting together my thoughts and vision for a franchise. Even though I had a young startup company and had very few resources, I believed we could really make a franchise happen.

On a long shot, I started a little primary research and looked on the back of the book and saw the picture of Erv Keup and his address. I was able to find his phone number with a little hard work and research (this was way before Google). I contacted his office and expected to leave a message. But, when I explained to his receptionist what we were trying to do, he immediately took my call and graciously spent over an hour talking to me about our franchise model and shared some money-saving tips and ideas to get us started. After we had a few phone conversations, Erv volunteered to drive over 100 miles to Santa Barbara, where I lived. But he didn't mind because of his passion for franchising and his enthusiasm for the potential of our model.

He was able to show us cost-effective ways to create our franchise model and was flexible with helping us put our franchise documents together.

We launched our franchise concept and had successful growth over several years. We never would have been able to do it without the professional guidance that Erv gave us, or the emotional support that he always offered.

Erv and I quickly became friends and started working on other franchise projects over the years. Erv took me under his wing and acted as my mentor. He taught me the business. I then started my own franchise development and consulting company, and with Erv's guiding hand, we were able to launch several franchise concepts over the years. The one constant throughout was Erv's friendship. We knew that when our wives were tired of hearing us talk about franchising, we could always call each other and spend hours talking about the ins and the outs of our industry.

At the end of 2010, as Erv entered into his retirement years, it was clear to me and other colleagues that he should be recognized by the franchise industry for his lifetime of work and support. I started working on a Lifetime Achievement Award for Erv several months before the end of 2011 in hopes of presenting it to him in November of that year. Unfortunately, we were all surprised and shocked when Erv suddenly took ill and passed away on October 16, 2011. Even on his deathbed, he was instructing his sons on how to finish the seventh edition of *Franchise Bible*. His passion for the franchise industry, the people who worked within it, and his overall belief in franchising and its contribution to the economy have helped countless people realize their dreams through business ownership.

While crafting ideas for the seventh edition, Erv told me that he really wanted to emphasize how and why franchising is such a huge part of the American lifestyle and such an integral part of the success of the American dream, and how it could be and indeed has been a big part of our current economic recovery.

Erv was most proud of his loving family. He would often tell me stories of their many adventures. He is survived by his wife Mary of 54 years, his 8 children, and his 17 grandchildren. He told me he often teased his kids that 17 grandchildren was a good start but if they followed his pattern he should have had 64. I had the privilege of attending his funeral service and getting to know other members of his family. They are a family of strong believers in God, and his service was a beautiful celebration of his life. Erv Keup practiced franchise law for over 45 years and helped countless franchisors and franchisees through the discovery and evaluation processes both personally with his firm and through the *Franchise Bible*. Goodbye, my friend. Thank you for being my mentor.

Erv was a great man and he'll be greatly missed. This lifetime achievement, remembering Erv Keup, is our dedication and memorial to a great franchise believer and to a man who was always there to aid others in the pursuit of their franchising dreams.

Preface

Before you enter into any business venture, you should fully understand your options in order to make an educated decision. Becoming a business owner is a huge decision with many variables to carefully consider. When you are contemplating business ownership, your options include buying a franchise, buying an existing business that is not a franchise, and starting a business from scratch. If you are looking to expand your existing business you have options as well. For example, you can franchise your business, open additional company-owned locations, or enter into other product or service distribution arrangements.

This book provides fundamental information on the subject of franchising and insight into what makes a franchise operation successful. Whether you are interested in franchising your business, buying a franchise, or growing an existing franchise organization as a franchisor or franchise owner, *Franchise Bible,* Eighth Edition, will be a valuable resource.

Read the Whole Book

We recommend that you read the entire book regardless of your current area of interest. For instance, someone who wants to franchise an existing business will find Part I of the book very informative even though it is geared toward those wanting to purchase a franchise and vice versa. The in-depth description of the franchise legal documents is located in Part I, Chapter 3.

You will be able to customize your experience to best serve your purpose and the type of business that you are involved with. You will find the book's companion website Franchise Bible Study (www.franchisebiblestudy. com) mentioned throughout the book. The site gives you interactive options to view additional materials, content, and video sessions from trainers and franchise experts. You can simply choose the content and exercises that apply to your situation and goals to best assist you in your business endeavors.

IN THE EIGHTH EDITION

Franchise Bible, Eighth Edition, is a multimedia experience with access to website and mobile app features. The book includes an interactive roadmap that allows each reader to customize what they read and access based on the reader's individual business circumstances and goals. Sections within the book will feature links to a number of online Franchise Bible Studies, such as expert videos, case studies, quizzes, downloads, interactive blogs, and much more. These resources will be accessible through computer and mobile devices.

New in this edition:

- All new, step-by-step, interactive roadmap for buying, launching, and growing a franchise.

- All new "Franchise Your Business" section with expert tutorials and tricks of the trade.
- All new "Grow Your Franchise" section for existing franchisors and franchise owners, featuring the Franchise Ten Commandments.
- Brand new www.franchisebiblestudy.com companion website featuring exercises and more to customize your reader experience to fit your business needs.
- New comprehensive exhibits including franchise terminology, veil of protection, and overview of North American Securities Administrators Association (NASAA).

PART I

Buying and Operating a Franchise

(Becoming a Franchise Owner)

The Basics of Franchising and the Changing Landscape of Franchise Marketing and Recruiting

Franchising has been around in some form at least since the 1800s. Though this business expansion and sales technique did not yet have the legal name or structure it does today, some companies in the United States were allowing others the right to use their names and logos to sell products and services in more remote parts of the country. In exchange, the owner of the new business would buy all of the equipment from the original company—of course—but they would also share a portion of the profit made from each sale.

Over the decades, this arrangement took on the formal name of *franchising* and also gathered both legitimate practitioners and fraudsters who used franchising to bilk the general public. As a result of the perceived widespread abuse, California passed groundbreaking legislation that for the first time regulated the franchise industry. Soon after California, the federal government passed its own regulations and charged the Federal Trade Commission (FTC) with the task of overseeing the burgeoning industry. In 1979, the FTC issued what in the industry became known as *the Rule*. Following on the heels of these two laws, several other states passed laws of their own to control franchising. These became known as the *registration states* because they require the franchisor to conform its offering to meet state law and in most cases demands that the franchisor register the offering before any sales efforts can start. We talk more about the registration states in later chapters.

In 2007, after over 12 years of work, *the Rule* was revised, and today we have the so-called *Revised Rule*. Though it kept many of the features of the original, it brought the law up-to-date in many important ways that we explore in this book.

What Franchising Is Today

Franchising, in modern business language, is a method of marketing through which successful *franchisors* (business owners) expand the retail distribution of their goods or services by contracting with *franchisees* (independent third parties). Franchisees agree to operate the retail sales or service outlets featuring the franchisor's original trademarked goods or services and agree to implement the franchisor's marketing methods at the franchisee's capital costs. In exchange for this opportunity, the franchisee agrees to pay an initial fee and ongoing royalties to the franchisor.

The FTC offers a more succinct legal definition of a "franchise." It states that a franchise is:

> . . . any continuing commercial relationship or arrangement,
> whatever it may be called, in which the terms of the offer or

contract specify, or the franchise seller promises or represents, orally or in writing, that:

1. The franchisee will obtain the right to operate a business that is identified or associated with the franchisor's trademark, or to offer, sell, or distribute goods, services, or commodities that are identified or associated with the franchisor's trademark;

2. The franchisor will exert or has authority to exert a significant degree of control over the franchisee's method of operation, or provide significant assistance in the franchisee's method of operation; and

3. As a condition of obtaining or commencing operation of the franchise, the franchisee makes a required payment or commits to make a required payment to the franchisor or its affiliate

The Revised Rule makes it clear that a business relationship between parties will be a franchise only if it meets all three elements. This is true in non-registration states as well as most of the registration states. Most of the registration states have adopted a similar definition, while others define a franchise using more expansive language.

Why Choose Franchising?

Very few people have the natural ability or expertise to be efficient at all aspects of running a successful business. That is where the franchisor's experience comes into play.

Franchise organizations offer a structure for launching, operating, and growing a business. Indeed, the successful franchisor will deliver the entire framework around which the business is built. Franchisors usually create comprehensive operations manuals and training programs for their franchise owners that cover marketing, operations, accounting, technology, and other areas that are specific to the particular business model. These efficiencies are designed to enable franchise owners to earn more and spend less time and effort than otherwise would be required to open and operate a similar business on their own.

COLLABORATION

The franchise organization model offers the franchisee the ability to grow under a common brand and share in the benefits of a larger group of business owners. Though each business is independently owned and managed, all franchisees share in the collaborative benefits of the organization through the support and oversight of the franchisor including:

- Group advertising resources not typically available to small independent business owners
- Owning your own business and making day-to-day decisions yourself, guided by the experience of a successful business enterprise
- The ability to sell products and services to markets that company-owned outlets have difficulty serving because of higher operational costs and lower motivation of employees in company-owned outlets
- The benefit of recognized and proven service marks, trademarks, proprietary information, patents, and/or designs
- Training from successful business operators
- A lower risk of failure and/or loss of investments than if you were to start your own business from scratch
- Being a part of a uniform operation, which means all franchises will share the same interior and exterior physical appearance, the same product, the same service and product quality, and overall customer brand awareness
- Operational support from the franchisor, both before and after launching your business venture, in areas such as financing, accounting, employee training, and operational procedures
- An opportunity to enhance your management abilities within an established business model that you could not experience in most employment situations

From the franchisor's perspective, this collaboration:
- Offers the franchisor a method of rapid expansion
- Spreads the brand messaging and awareness over a large network of franchise owners
- Taps in to the franchise owner community's "pride of ownership"
- Allows the franchise owner community to grow due to a duplicable system and support
- Features increased buying power for goods and services due to higher volume with suppliers
- Enables new products and services to be developed in the field with more testing and input
- Provides a steady cash flow to the franchisor to facilitate overall growth of the system
- Can fund the brand recognition effort to grow nationally and globally

FRANCHISING OFFERS A BETTER CHANCE TO SUCCEED

The U.S. Department of Commerce and other authors of statistics concerning franchising have shown that the revenue from franchise establishments accounts for over one-third of all U.S. retail sales.

According to studies on the economic impact of franchises, franchise businesses produce over 3 percent of nonfarm private output in the United States, and when the total contribution of franchise businesses was considered (which includes the goods and services used or purchased by franchise businesses and their employees), franchise businesses account for approximately 9 percent of nonfarm private output in the United States.

Government research over the years has indicated that the success rate for franchise-owned endeavors is significantly better than the rate for non-franchise-owned small businesses. In short, the good news is that franchising makes up a significant part of the national economy and presents a statistically better chance for success than other business options. Of course, there are no guarantees, and not every franchise is a surefire way to multiply your savings and provide you with an enjoyable occupation.

THE FREEDOM FACTOR

Most individuals seek three common elements when choosing a franchised business:

- Flexibility
- Money
- Status

These three elements are important for a variety of reasons and seem to be common denominators when people seek a new business as a career path. *Flexibility* has always been a hot button for entrepreneurs who exchange the stability of a "real job" for the freedom that comes with being their own boss. *Money*, or income, is always a factor, but surprisingly is seldom the most important. We know many people who have left huge salaries behind because they were miserable, to pursue the American Dream and launch a business. *Status* is an all-encompassing category that includes not only titles and position, but more importantly, the feeling of purpose one has and being a part of something significant.

Owning a franchise can provide you with all three of these elements if you operate the business successfully and manage your time and resources properly.

HAPPY FRANCHISE OWNERS MAKE MORE MONEY

It has been said that if you love what you do, you can't help but succeed. There is a lot of truth to this statement. If you can align yourself with a franchise that really fits, you will be much happier, which in turn results in higher productivity. This is a simple philosophy that is often overlooked. Some franchise organizations have suffered because they lost sight of this reality during the fast growth stages.

The explosive growth that many franchises experience is referred to as "hockey stick" growth due to the way it is charted on a line graph. Sometimes companies are so successful and grow so fast that they seemingly forget about the little things that made them successful in the first place. In this case, their initial success can lead to their ultimate failure. A franchise organization that forgets that their franchise-owner community is in fact their "customer" base (each of whom should be treated with respect and with an eye towards making them satisfied) usually comes down like a house of cards.

Think about this for just a moment: If the franchisor understands that its franchisees are the heart and soul of their success and understand a very basic premise—if the franchisees are happy then they will generate more revenue—then it will build on that reputation and financial model. But if the franchisor sees its franchisees merely as cogs in a wheel that deserve no respect, the system ultimately fails—and not because the end product is poor, but because the sales force that is presenting the product to the general public is dissatisfied. We see this all too often.

As you evaluate franchise organizations, be sure to investigate their commitment to their franchise owners, as well as their future development plans to enable their franchisees enjoy continued growth and success. We discuss this in more detail in later chapters.

The Changing Landscape of Franchise Marketing and Recruiting

In the franchise world, franchisors use the term *recruiting* instead of *selling* because prospects are being chosen vs. being sold something—even though franchisees pay for a franchise opportunity. Franchisors must be selective as they accept new franchise owners into their franchise communities. It is counterproductive to award a franchise to an individual who is not a good fit. The franchisor should award a franchise based on the candidate's compatibility with the system generally, and should look specifically at the candidate's maturity, business acumen, willingness to learn, and ability to follow a system.

In the last decade, franchisors have undergone a huge evolution in the way that they communicate their marketing and recruiting messages to prospective franchisees. This is due to the free availability of information on the Internet and related advances in technology. As a prospective franchise owner in today's world, you are among the most advanced and informed buyers in the history of franchising.

This section describes how franchise marketing and recruiting have evolved and how you, the potential franchisee, can take an educated approach as you navigate through the discovery and research process with the goal of identifying the best franchise business for your family and you. It is the franchisor's job to adequately educate potential franchise buyers, through their marketing efforts, to attract the best candidates. This increases the organization's overall success potential, which benefits everyone involved.

The Five Pillars of Marketing

The traditional methods of marketing franchise opportunities and recruiting franchisees during the pre-internet years looked much like other business models of that time. This included what we call *The Five Pillars of Marketing* that make up the primary categories of the marketing umbrella.

Think of *marketing* as the general term that we use to describe all of the efforts that businesses use to attract buyers—be it grocers and their customers, or franchisors that are seeking franchisees. Marketing can be broken down into the following five categories: advertising, sales, direct mail, public relations, and promotions, which we will refer to as "the five pillars of marketing," as visualized in Figure 1-1. These categories, then, are broken down into marketing campaigns.

Figure 1-1. The Five Pillars of Marketing

ADVERTISING

Traditional franchise advertising once focused on TV, radio, and publications such as franchise magazines and catalogs, business magazines, local newspapers, and billboards. The franchise buyer could view ads featuring franchise opportunities for sale and could also read articles and testimonials. The franchisors controlled the content and the messages, which limited the buyer's perception of the business to what the franchisor presented to them.

Today's advertisements are still placed in the traditional form but tend to have a much different call to action. Instead of "Call Now," the ads direct the reader to the franchisor's website where they can learn more and engage via email with the franchisor's development department. This is less threatening than a phone call while still providing a heightened level of interaction with the franchisor. Online advertisements are very popular as well. We explore this further in the following section.

Today you will find more local TV commercials touting the sale of all goods and services—including of course business opportunities and franchises—as the cable providers and similar mediums continue to lower their costs. Interactive TV commercials are also becoming more popular in many markets. These commercials allow you to request information or order a product or service by pressing a button on your remote control. Franchise opportunities that utilize this platform may be showing their commitment to growth by using modern technology.

SALES

Good old-fashioned salesmanship has always been a big part of the franchise-marketing world. Buying and starting a business is typically one of the biggest decisions in a person's life. Franchise buyers tend to do a great deal of research before they choose the best business match. The franchisor's sales department is responsible for educating the prospective franchise owner as they move through the discovery process.

Independent franchise consultants and brokers have become an extension of the franchisor's sales department. They invest in their own marketing and recruiting efforts to identify prospective franchise buyers. They then introduce them to franchisors that match their franchise system's criteria. In many cases, the buyer will experience a more balanced discovery process if they are working with a consultant or broker because they offer their clients education and resources.

Live events, such as franchise expositions or local franchise seminars, are other sales methods that many franchisors participate in. These events give the franchisor's sales representatives the opportunity to meet face-to-face with many prospective buyers at one time. In turn the franchise buyers can compare a variety of opportunities side by side, saving the prospective franchisee a lot of time.

Audio recordings and videos are also effective methods for sales communication. Franchisors can feature their concept overview and testimonials on DVD or on their websites. With these methods, franchisors can professionally showcase their concept, and buyers can "shop and compare" a variety of franchise concepts at their convenience.

Live web presentations have become a very cost-effective sales presentation tool. Franchisors can host scheduled or impromptu online meetings with interested buyers. The presenter can use various tools such as presentation slides, website content, or other web-based documents or files that can appear on the prospective franchisees' computers as they listen to the presentation. This method also provides participants the opportunity to personally ask questions and the opportunity to hear answers to questions he or she may not have considered.

As you research various franchise opportunities, you will want to make sure that the sales department (or the independent consultant or broker) is doing their job of providing balanced information and education about the opportunity without pressuring you. With smaller startup franchises, you may be dealing directly with the founder of the company. You can learn a great deal about a franchise if they have an effective sales system that utilizes the tools outlined above.

DIRECT MARKETING

Direct marketing includes email, newsletters, and mailers. Direct mail has for decades been a very effective marketing and recruiting method. It allows franchisors to stand out from their competitors with a strong message in a postcard or sales-letter format. Such marketing has become more advanced with the introduction of online mailing list services. These services can identify individuals who fit the criteria the franchisor is looking for based on demographics and buying habits. For instance, you may receive a direct-mail piece from an automotive franchise if you frequent certain automotive websites or subscribe to automotive magazines.

Some franchisors have developed a newsletter program for existing franchisees and even for prospective franchise owners. You may be able to sign up on their website to receive their newsletters. This gives you some insight into their company culture and franchise community and is a great way to see if you would fit in. Remember that merely having a set of skills does not mean that you would fit into any opportunity. As we've noted, the culture of the franchisor, the method by which they do business, and the way that they communicate with prospective franchisees must all be weighed when making the buying decision.

PUBLIC RELATIONS

Public relations or PR campaigns can take many forms. PR campaigns are often "good will" efforts that a company makes to show it is involved with their communities. It may be as simple as the company sponsoring a non-profit organization, or as extravagant as creating a philanthropic movement of its own.

You can learn a lot about a company by the types of PR efforts it participates in. Research the company's PR history to ensure that your values are in line with its philanthropic vision. You may find publicity articles that highlight the company's efforts. You will want to confirm that the company is genuinely supporting certain causes for the good of the cause and not just for the exposure.

PROMOTIONS

A promotion is any "out of the ordinary" campaign or event to attract new business or increase awareness of a company. This can be as simple as a special sale or incentive program. You may also see larger efforts such as customer loyalty programs, customer appreciation events, or rewards programs.

In the franchise world, it is common to be invited to attend a franchisor's "discovery day" or "decision day" event. These events will allow you to meet the franchisor's executive and support team, to learn more about their business, and even meet with existing franchise owners.

The Sixth Pillar: The Internet

Even though you will find elements of the original five pillars of marketing within the internet platform, the internet has become unique enough to be considered a standalone sixth pillar of marketing (see Figure 1-2). This section will help you identify the best practices for researching franchise opportunities by utilizing technology and the internet.

Not too many years ago, the "big boys," or well-known franchisors, had a competitive advantage because they had far more money and resources to market their franchise opportunities. Back then, the marketing and media options were very expensive, and emerging franchisors were priced out of the competition. The internet has leveled the playing field with much lower barriers of entry, thereby giving the advantage to creative companies—not just to those with large bank accounts.

Figure 1-2. Marketing today includes a sixth pillar—the internet.

WEBSITES

Franchisor's websites should be professional and educational. A buyer should be able to easily access information about the company's culture, products, and services.

Look for the following when you are evaluating a franchisor's website:

- Does the website look professional compared to the competitor's?
- Is the site easy to navigate and do you find valuable information about the opportunity?
- Does the franchisor address your primary concerns and questions upfront?
- Does the franchisor disclose the initial investment, or do they dance around this information?
- Is the website "mobile friendly" and easy to navigate and use on your mobile phone and tablet devices?

EMAIL

Once you have identified a few possible franchise opportunities, engage them on all technology levels to see how they respond. Those that are on top of their game, whether large or small, should respond reasonably quickly. Those franchisors that don't respond quickly (or at all) may be too strapped for cash to have invested in a solid marketing platform, may be too new to the industry to understand its marketing needs, or may simply be too lazy to operate in a business-like manner. Such franchisors end up getting so caught up in the idea of the franchise concept that they fail to see how to build the business in the first place.

The bottom line is that a buyer should never have to pursue a franchisor. A good rule of thumb is the reality that a franchisor's communication seldom gets better after you buy in to a franchise organization; if they can't get it right when they are wooing you as a new franchisee, they will not get it right when dealing with you as a franchise owner.

> When you send an email request, such as the one in Figure 1-3, you should receive a response within one day. It can be a good test to see how responsive and structured a franchisor will be.

Figure 1-3. Sample inquiry email to a franchisor

SAMPLE EMAIL REQUEST

Ms. Dodd,

Thank you for your quick response to my questions below. I am very interested in this franchise opportunity and look forward to learning more.

1. What is the estimated timeline between signing the franchise agreement and our grand opening?
2. I would like my brother to be a partner. Will he have to sign any documents?

> 3. Should I get in touch with financing companies and commercial real estate brokers now or should I do this after we sign up?
>
> Thank you again, Angela

Again, the savvy franchisor will be ready to quickly respond with answers to your questions and with additional information to entice you to take additional steps in the sales process.

BLOGS

Blogs offer a plethora of information about franchise opportunities. You can search the internet for relevant articles about the franchises you are interested in. Blogs also allow you to comment and ask questions of all of the blog participants. This allows you to experience a more interactive discovery process.

Take what you read on blogs with a grain of salt. Remember that just about anyone can comment on some blogs, so opinions and advice may, or may not, be credible. You can see trends in most cases that you may find helpful.

WEB PRESENTATIONS

Modern franchisors offer web presentations, web meetings, or webinars to present the features, advantages, and benefits that they have to offer. This platform is very convenient because you can participate in what is usually a live presentation from anywhere in the world.

Internet and Social Media

Today you have more access to influential people via social media, such as Facebook, Twitter, LinkedIn, and others, than ever before. First, identify the franchise opportunities you are interested in. Then, go to the franchisors' websites, if available. The web page may provide links to social media sites, which in turn will allow you to sneak a peek at the general tenor of social media's take on the franchisor. Don't be afraid to use social media yourself to engage the franchisor as it is yet another research opportunity and "test" opportunity. How quickly do they respond? What is the content of the response? What do other followers have to say about the franchisor's response? Often you can experience a more interactive dialog with the franchisor, their franchisees, and their customers if you use social media and the communication tools on social media sites.

You can join a variety of social media groups that focus on entrepreneurial and franchise topics. Websites such as Facebook and LinkedIn offer groups and discussion forums that focus specifically on franchising and business growth. Join these groups and don't be afraid to ask questions. Engage the franchisors, franchise owners, and individuals considering the purchase of a franchise. You will learn a great deal from the people who participate in these groups.

Social media allows all outsiders and insiders alike to engage in an ongoing personal conversation about the subject. You can gain a great deal of information by participating in various social media platforms, such as the Twitter conversation shown in Figure 1-4. You can use up to 140 characters (including spaces) per tweet.

Figure 1-4. Connecting with a franchisor on Twitter

TWITTER COMMENTS

@LelaG: Hello to those interested in the Noah's Ark Franchise. I am looking into this. So far it looks good. What do you think of a franchise like this one?

@Hannah_Noah's Ark [franchisor]: Hi @LelaG. Thanks for your interest. We will assist you in your efforts to research our business model. Feel free to call me to discuss.

@SamJoeArt: Very good question @LelaG. Good to see that

Noah's Ark is so responsive. I am looking into this franchise, too. What do you think?

@LelaG: Hi @SamJoeArt. I saw an awesome review Tweet from @MazieG today who said she is doing so well that she is opening another location soon.

@AddiePants: Are there any available territories in the Dallas area?

@Hannah_Noah's Ark [franchisor]: Hi @AFG2011: We do have one territory in metro Dallas in the north side of the city. Could that work for you?

@AddiePants: Thanks Hannah. That could work. I am not too far from that part of the city.

@Hannah_Noah's Ark [franchisor]: Hi @LelaG, @SamJoeArt and @AFG 20011. Join me for a web presentation this Wednesday at 6:30 MT. www.sample.com to register.

@NickBailey: My sister purchased one of these and loves it. She is making great money and enjoys her work every day. She feels like she is giving back. It sounds good to me.

@NickBailey: Can I join the web presentation too?

@Hannah_Noah's Ark [franchisor]: Hi @NickBailey. Sure you can join us. Click on this link to register www.sample.com.

@Sweetface1990: I would like to join in as well if there is still time.

> @Hannah_ Noah's Ark [franchisor]: Hi @Sweetface1990. You cer-
> tainly may join us. Click on this link www.sample.com to register
> or feel free to call me at 555-555-5555. Thanks.

As you can see in Figure 1-4, you have the opportunity to engage a community of individuals that share a common interest in the franchise that you are researching. This allows the franchisor to prove themselves by being responsive and informative as well.

ELECTRONIC NEWSLETTERS (E-NEWSLETTERS)

When available, you can sign up for electronic newsletters from franchisors you are interested in. You will glean insights into their company and find out what makes them tick. Their newsletters should be consistent and educational.

SEARCH ENGINE OPTIMIZATION (SEO)

Savvy franchisors are investing in search engine optimization efforts (SEO). They will do the research to identify the search history of the individuals who are attracted to their franchise opportunity. You can type keywords or keyword phrases (groups of keywords) into search engines to find franchises that align with your interests. The franchise opportunities that rank high in the "organic search" results tend to be the companies that have the best SEO programs and relevant website content. These companies can be considered more technology savvy. The organic results appear in order of relevance to your keywords when you perform a web search.

SEARCH ENGINE MARKETING (SEM)

Many franchises are marketed on the internet via search engine marketing. This includes organic results from search engines that in turn identify the companies with the most effective SEM. SEM also includes "pay" options like pay-per-click or banner advertisements.

RETARGETING ADVERTISING

Behavioral retargeting, remarketing, or simply retargeting is a form of online targeted advertising by which online advertising is targeted to consumers based on their previous internet actions. This technology places an already familiar brand in front of the potential buyer multiple times as they navigate the internet, resulting in more brand impressions and opportunities to buy.

TEXTING

Texting is fast becoming the biggest communication tool in use. Franchisors should be comfortable with communicating via text messaging. Ask up front if you can communicate via text as it may provide a more efficient and dynamic communication tool for interacting with franchisors and obtaining information. It has been proven that people respond to text messages faster than email or voicemail.

> Texting can fast-track various steps in your discovery and launch process. Discuss this with your contact at the franchisor's headquarters in advance so you don't lose valuable time.

Figure 1-5. Connecting with a franchisor via text message

SAMPLE TEXT MESSAGE

Hello Mr. Ramirez. I am meeting with my banker right now and we need the bottom-line figures for our required signage for our Noah's Ark franchise located on Fifth and Main for the loan package.

Hello Pablo. Our Franchise Disclosure document at Item 7 states $5,500 for the signage package. Let me know if you need anything else. Larry.

PODCASTS

You may find that there are podcasts about the franchises that interest you. Podcasts are online audio and/or video broadcasts on the internet. Podcasting franchisors present their franchise opportunity in more detail using this type of media. You can search for and subscribe to podcasts in applications like iTunes and in mobile apps like Stitcher.

SMART DEVICE APPLICATIONS

You can now search various smart devices for business opportunities and franchises. If you do so, be sure to investigate the franchisor's history and the depth of their technology.

Many franchise companies have launched smart device or apps for their customers' use. You can learn a lot about the level of professionalism and technology sophistication of a company by downloading its apps and trying them out for yourself. Evaluate the experience as a customer first and see how you feel about your future customers using the app for your business.

FUTURE TECHNOLOGIES

Some say that most of the technology we will use ten years from now has yet to be invented. Franchisors that want to attract more technology-based franchise buyers must commit to delivering the most cutting-edge products, services, and technology available or risk falling behind. In selecting a franchise opportunity, you may want to consider the technological tools and marketing efficiency of the franchisor as it can be an indicator of an effective franchise operation.

Conclusion

As a franchise buyer nowadays, you have more information at your fingertips than at any other time in history. Use the tools, tips, and techniques in this chapter to fully investigate the franchise opportunities you are interested in. Remember that the key to success in the franchise business is a good fit between the franchisor and the franchise owners. Good luck in your new endeavor!

CHAPTER 2

Choosing the Right Franchise Opportunity

Are you currently working for someone but longing to be your own boss and to own your own business? Maybe you're retired and looking for a way to get back into the business world? Are you a recent college graduate or military veteran who wants to get into your own business?

There are many ways to get into franchising. This chapter is intended to help you narrow the field of options and help you create a sound search method that in turn will give you the greatest chance to succeed.

Check Out the Companion Website

Chapter 1 provides a good understanding of the franchise basics and the different methods of interacting with various franchisors's marketing departments. Feel free to go to www. franchisebiblestudy.com to access your customizable *Franchise Bible* reader's experience and take the first steps to build your franchise roadmap. Have a great journey!

Why Buy a Franchise Instead of Going It Alone?

Most new franchise owners have little experience in business ownership. Millions of dollars have been lost over the years by new business owners who simply didn't know what to do when they encountered obstacles. "I don't know what I don't know" has significant meaning and is a common feeling among many new business owners.

The franchisor, on the other hand, has "been through the ringer" and has already made most of the mistakes that a new business owner would otherwise suffer. As a result, they have a system, policies, procedures, marketing, and technology to help the new franchisee through the startup phase. In many cases, participating in a franchised business should enable you to quickly recoup your initial *franchise fee* (the fee you pay the franchisor in exchange for being awarded the franchise opportunity) by saving you money on such things as location selection, build-out methods, back office solutions, and discounted inventory purchases.

Additionally you should realize ways to make more money through meaningful training and marketing programs that you would otherwise have to figure out on your own. Though it is true that in all business ventures a risk of failure exists, according to statistics provided by the U.S. Department of Commerce, the chances of success in a franchise operation are generally better than those of a business started from scratch or even purchased as an existing business. And surprisingly, the autonomy required to operate a franchise is not necessarily less than in operating a business you start from scratch or one you purchase. Your franchisor should help you make more money and spend less, which increases your profit.

Am I a Good Franchise Candidate?

It's not for everyone. This is no less true in franchising than it is in medicine, teaching, or gardening. Thus, to help you make this determination you must ask yourself some questions:

- *What do you really enjoy doing?* This does not have to be the work that you are doing at the moment. Instead it could be a hobby that you are passionate about. Indeed, one of the most important factors that may determine your success or failure is the level of enjoyment and satisfaction you can hope to experience in operating the franchise from day to day. You must be involved with the daily operation of your business at some level regardless of the model you choose. So it is critical for you to "inventory yourself" to make sure you are indeed a good franchise candidate.

- *Do you like working with the public?* If the answer is no, there may still be "business-to-business" franchise opportunities that require you to work with other business people, but the truth is that you are still working with the public.

- *Do you like the idea of being the boss?* It was President Truman who said "The Buck Stops Here," and the burden of being the boss cannot be more succinctly stated. You are responsible for the daily grind that is business: book keeping, employment issues, inventory control, and the like. Though you may delegate these duties to an employee, ultimately, it will be your job to ensure that it is all done in the manner that the franchisor requires.

- *Are you willing to have employees?* Though it is not exactly working with the public, the ability to work with employees in a positive manner is no less important than your ability to work with your customers. If hiring, directing, and firing employees is not your thing, then you may look for a business that does not require employees.

- *Are you willing to take direction from the franchisor when setting up and operating the business?* As strange as it may sound, entrepreneurs are not the best franchisees! A franchisor does not want someone that will learn the system and then take off on tangents that are not within the confines of system. Time and again it has been confirmed that it is the franchisee that can follow the system that is successful. Deviating from it is counterproductive, in violation of your franchise contract, and more often than not, results in a failed franchise.
- *Is your family enthusiastic about the idea of buying a franchise?* Will you enjoy working with them if they are going to work in the business?
- *Do you have the necessary capital resources?* Can you make the financial sacrifices?
- Are you emotionally prepared for working the hours required to succeed? Succeeding in franchising requires hard work and sometimes long hours.

Don't be afraid to ask friends and acquaintances for their opinions on your abilities along these lines. And don't rely on just one opinion—get several. To help you in such an evaluation, use the checklist in Figure 2-1.

Figure 2-1. Franchisee Suitability Checklist

CHECKLIST FOR EVALUATING YOUR SUITABILITY AS A FRANCHISEE

Carefully consider these questions before buying your own franchise. A majority of "yes" answers indicate that franchise ownership could be a very good direction for you.

YES	NO	
☐	☐	Have you and your spouse and/or business partner(s) discussed the pros and cons of going into business for yourselves?
☐	☐	Are you in complete agreement to move forward?
☐	☐	Do you have the financial resources required to buy a franchise? If not, do you have a plan or resources to get the capital?
☐	☐	Are you ready to make the sacrifices and time investment necessary to operate a franchise?
☐	☐	Will the possible loss of employment benefits be outweighed by the potential monetary and personal rewards that come from owning your own business?
☐	☐	Have you made a thorough, written balance sheet of your assets and liabilities, as well as liquid cash resources?
☐	☐	Do you and your business partner(s) have family support for this new venture?
☐	☐	Are you comfortable with the fact that most new businesses, including franchises, generally do not break even for at least one year after opening?
☐	☐	Are you able to handle the emotional and physical responsibilities involved in operating a franchise?
☐	☐	Are you prepared to give up some independence of action in exchange for the advantages the franchise offers you?
☐	☐	Have you really examined the type of franchise or business you desire and truthfully concluded that you would enjoy running it for several years or until retirement?
☐	☐	Are you and your business partners in good enough health to launch and grow a new business at this time?
☐	☐	Do you have the ability and experience to work with your franchisor, your employees, and your customers?

❏ ❏ Have you asked your friends and relatives for their candid opinions as to your emotional, mental, and physical suitability to running your own business?

❏ ❏ Do you have a capable, willing heir to take over the business if you become disabled?

❏ ❏ Do you have past experience in business that will qualify you for the particular type of franchise or business you desire?

❏ ❏ Have you conducted independent research on the industry you are contemplating entering?

❏ ❏ If you have made your choice of franchises, have you researched the background and experience of your prospective franchisor?

❏ ❏ Does the product or service you propose to sell have a market in your prospective territory at the prices you will have to charge?

❏ ❏ Will there be a market for your product or service five years from now?

❏ ❏ Do you feel that you can beat the competition that exists in your prospective territory already?

❏ ❏ Do you know an experienced, business-oriented franchise attorney who can evaluate the franchise contract you are considering?

❏ ❏ Do you know an experienced, business-minded accountant?

❏ ❏ Have you prepared a business plan for the franchise or business of your choice?

It is true that franchising gives you a greater chance to succeed in business than going on your own. However, we want to dispense with the most persistent myth about franchising: that the franchisee can make a lot of money from the franchised business with a minimum of effort. This has never been the case, and it is a serious misconception. As is true in most things in life, the franchisee who works the hardest profits the most from a franchise business.

Initially at least, you must be able to make sacrifices:

- *Be prepared to put in long hours of hard work.* It is not unusual for the boss to be the first one to arrive in the morning and the last one to leave at night.

- *Be prepared to understand and be able to carry out all of the jobs required to operate the business.* This might include janitor, to cook, and CEO. If an employee fails to show up for work, at least in the beginning, it is often the owner who must fill in the gap.

- *Be prepared to be disappointed.* Understand that you will occasionally be disappointed by an employee's performance, which may require you to discipline or even fire them. This is never an easy task, but it's one that comes with the territory.

- *Be prepared to be the most organized person in the business.* Everyone in the business will look to you to organize the operations—be it those necessary to run the day-to-day operations or close out the business year's books and records.

- *Be financially and emotionally prepared for setbacks.* Every business that has ever existed has had to overcome difficulties. Businesses cycle through ups and downs, have difficulty with inventory control, and suffer the hardship of finding competent help. These are par for the course. Having the franchisor in your corner will certainly give you a great resource to help with these issues, but in the end, it is you who must resolve them.

You must select a particular field of business you like—or better, that you have a passion for (like working with cars, say, or working with numbers) and then decide whether that endeavor is suitable given your past experience and talents. If you have a background in mechanical engineering and enjoy working with equipment, then a vehicle-based franchise opportunity may be the franchise sector you should consider. Has your experience always been in bookkeeping? Looking into accounting-based franchises may be the way to go. On the other hand, if you are an individual who loves working with food, then looking into the restaurant industry may be an interesting exercise.

Although finding a line of work that you can enjoy is important, you want to make sure that the business is a solid model with an existing market of potential customers. Choose the business in which you can excel so you can have the freedom to enjoy the fun things in life. Once you have used this section to narrow the field of opportunities, you can pursue a more established course of action often called the *discovery process*.

The Discovery Process

This section breaks down the process used to find the franchise opportunities that best fit your skill set, experience, and goals.

1. DEFINE YOUR GOALS

What are the reasons that caused you to consider franchise ownership in the first place? They can include the desire to be your own boss, the desire to better balance work and family, the interest in using your own skills to build your net worth, and other similar factors. Be brutally honest. This is the time to look deep into yourself to locate your true desires. Setting goals is an important starting point for your business.

> A business without goals is like a ship without a rudder—it will wander off course.

Franchise Bible Study: Download the Goal Setting Exercise and get started on your business goals.

Many people set goals only to fall short and give up. This reinforces negative feelings instead of resulting in positive achievement. You can apply the following three goal rules to increase your success:

- *A goal must be realistic and attainable.* Challenging is good, but you will quickly lose interest if it is out of reach.
- *A goal must be specific and measurable.* "I want to be rich someday" is neither. "I will have 1,000,000 in the bank by the time I turn 50" is better.

- *A goal must be something that you want.* Nobody can give you a meaningful goal but you.

2. IDENTIFY FRANCHISE OPTIONS

Do your homework to identify an initial group of franchise opportunities that meet some or all of your criteria. It is good to have at least a few options to compare. Look into franchises that interest you and ones that you can see yourself running. Consider the "day-in-the-life" of the operators to make sure that you can visualize yourself in their place.

The first place most people search for franchise opportunities is online. This method can be somewhat frustrating due to the vast number of options available. It is also challenging to discern between different types of franchises. Narrow the field by evaluating what type of business and investment range are compatible with your lifestyle before you begin your internet search. At this point, you may also choose to work with a qualified franchise broker to help you narrow the field and assist you through the discovery process. Most brokers work on commission paid by the franchisor. Make sure that the broker has a good track record and experience in the franchise industry. They may be able to help you with financing, site selection, and other elements of your business launch. If you use a broker, they should help and advise you through the balance of the discovery process.

3. INITIAL CONTACT

See how the franchisor handles your inquiries. If you get sent to voicemail, note how long it takes for them to return your call. Don't hesitate to ask to talk to different members of their organizations to get a feel for their company cultures. Keep track of how the initial communication with the franchisors play out:

- Did they answer the phone live with a professional greeting?
- Were you able to talk to someone in the franchise sales department immediately on the first call attempt?
- Did they answer all of your questions to your satisfaction?

- Did they ask for your information?
- Were they courteous, professional, and interested in you and your needs?
- Did they offer the next steps? That is, did they send you information?
- How do you rate them each on a scale of 1 to 10 (ten being best)?

4. IDENTIFY THEIR PROCESSES

When you contact a franchisor, ask them to outline their franchise sales and qualifying processes. This will help you stay on track and ensure progress. Be wary of companies that do not seem to have any systems or process for you to follow. A franchise opportunity should be all about systems, on all fronts.

5. EVALUATE THE FRANCHISE DOCUMENTS

The next chapter goes into a detailed review of the franchise disclosure document (FDD) and the franchise agreement in the next chapter. Once you receive the FDD, it is a good idea to have a qualified franchise attorney review the franchise disclosure documents with you. A standard business attorney may have little or no experience in franchising and could end up costing you more money and time since they will need to learn the industry.

6. INTERVIEW EXISTING FRANCHISE OWNERS

The franchise owner list must be included in the FDD. If it is missing, it is an incomplete document. Contact the franchise owners to see how they are doing. We discuss this more fully in the "Interviewing Franchisees" section later in this chapter.

7. ATTEND DISCOVERY DAY

Most franchisors hold regular discovery or decision day events. This gives you a chance to visit their headquarters and meet their team. These events are opportunities for both the franchisor and you to really size up the potential business relationship. Make no mistake: They are looking closely at your personality, your manner of dress, and all of the other social cues that exist whenever you first meet someone. You, of course, should do the same. As they must feel comfortable with you, you must be comfortable with them. Remember that you may be in business with them for five or even 20 years, depending on the franchise opportunity. This is a decision that must sit comfortably with you on an emotional level as well as a business and financial level.

8. EXECUTE THE FRANCHISE AGREEMENT

The very last step is to execute the franchise agreement and related documents attached to it. Be sure to file your copy of the executed documents for future reference.

Interviewing Existing Franchise Owners (Franchisees)

The single most informative discovery tool at your disposal for any franchise opportunity is interviewing current and former franchisees. Talking with them is a critical component of the prospective franchisee's due diligence. In order to help you through what can sometimes be a nerve-wracking process, we have prepared a list of questions that will act as a starting point for such conversations.

Start this process by first finding the list of current and former franchisees that must be an exhibit to the FDD. In statistics, one finds the greatest accuracy from the largest pool of contributors. The same holds true here. Your goal will be to contact as many franchisees both current and past as you can. In doing so, you will pick up on trends and be able to identify common threads throughout the comments. If there seem to be too many to manage, start with the franchisees that are closest to you geographically and move outward to the next city, state, or region.

Call as many former franchisees that you can. Though many may not want to talk with you or may tell you only negative things, such conversations are valuable and, once again, may provide a common theme that will help you make your final business decision.

Remember that franchisees are running a business. Don't call and expect them to drop everything and talk with you at that moment. Respect their time, as you would ask others to respect your time. If you can set up an appointment to talk on the phone, that would be the proper thing to do. If you can meet with them personally that would be even better. Remember, in some cases, busy franchise owners may not be able to talk with you.

Be honest about the purpose of your call. And be honest in your responses. The purpose of the calls is to have a conversation and not an interrogation.

Consider the following questions:

- How long have you owned your franchise?
- Do you own more than one, or do you have plans to own more?
- Did you use a franchise attorney or accountant to help you?
- What was your professional background before you purchased your franchise?
- Did your prior experience help or hinder your business operations?
- Was the training what you expected?
- Were the manuals helpful? Do you still use them?
- Did the franchisor do what they promised before you opened?
- Did the franchisor do what they promised after you opened?
- Has the franchisor been reasonably available to help with problems?
- Are you working the hours you expected?
- Are you earning the money that you expected?
- What financial goal is realistic as a single-unit franchise owner?
- Do you believe that you can meet your financial goals in the future?
- What can the franchisor do to help you reach your goals? Do you believe that they will?

- What would you change about the business?
- Knowing what you know now, would you do it again?
- What advice would you give me?

This is not an exhaustive list by any means. Some of these questions may not be appropriate for some franchisees, whereas other questions may arise as a result of your conversations. Don't be afraid to improvise or go off script. As with any conversation, what starts out going one direction will often end on a totally different path. Write down comprehensive notes so you can compare and identify any reoccurring themes or patterns.

Quit the Team and Join the Party

We have all been subjected to team-building exercises, such as falling backwards off a chair into the arms of our faithful colleagues. The question is, does this really build team spirit between co-workers?

In the franchise world, we don't have the same organizational structure that most businesses have. Franchise owners are spread out all over the map, and the franchisor does the best job they can to assist them on a global basis. In other words, the team is never on the field at the same time or place.

Every day, franchise owners around the world get up in the morning, put on their company colors, and hit the streets to build their businesses. They have numerous colleagues doing the same, but it often doesn't feel like it.

When you join a franchise organization, or party, you can realize the benefits of a business group that truly works together for the common good of all.

When you are evaluating and interviewing franchise

> Franchise owners are more of a party than a team. A *party* is a group of people that share the same beliefs and values and have a common belief in the organization's mission. Think of a search party, political party, or even a celebration party. Franchise owners buy in to the vision of the franchisor. They "join the party" when they invest in a particular franchise model.

organizations, meet with as many of their executive, management, and support team members as you can. Ask them questions to confirm the common beliefs and vision of the company. Make sure you feel good about being a part of their organization, or "party," before you commit to joining them.

Buying an Existing Franchise

The big difference between purchasing a franchise from a franchisor and purchasing a franchise from an existing franchisee is that, if it is truly a sale by a franchisee, the franchisee is not bound by restrictions on revealing actual or projected revenue figures. By the same token, the franchisee/seller is also not bound by any legal disclosure requirements, such as those issued by the Federal Trade Commission.

Ensure that you secure a written purchase agreement in which the franchisee who is selling the franchise produces accurate, truthful financial statements and warrants their veracity. Because the business is also a franchise, familiarize yourself with the terms and conditions of the franchise agreement and with the information in the franchisor's disclosure document as well as any transfer restrictions or fees.

Conclusion

At this point you should have a pretty good idea whether franchising is the best business model for you and your family. You should also have narrowed the field of options down to your top few. You can now continue your *Franchise Bible* Study roadmap as you move forward.

Legal Considerations

One of the unique elements of the franchise model is the legal disclosure and contractual structure that binds franchisors and franchisees together. You may be new to the franchise business model and may be seeing franchise documents for the first time. This chapter will give you an in-depth overview of the franchise legal structure and related documents to help you navigate the process.

Understanding the Franchise Documents

Franchisors in the United States work under what may be the most complete set of governmental regulation of franchising in the world. In 1979, the Federal Trade Commission (FTC) was charged by the United States Congress with the task of policing franchising at the national level. At that time, it created the law entitled Disclosure Requirements and Prohibitions Concerning Franchising and Business Opportunity Ventures (known informally as the Rule). In 2007, after twelve years of work, the FTC revised the Rule into what we call the Revised Rule.

In addition, the franchisor must consider the registration and disclosure statutes, rules, and regulations of some 15 states (with four more states requiring a form of exemption filing). Often called the *registration states*, each one has separate laws that specifically talk about franchising. Go to www.entrepreneur.com/franchiseresources for the list of registration states.

In the registration states, the franchisor must comply with the Revised Rule *and* with the state-based statutes. In the non-registration states, the franchisor is required to abide only by the Revised Rule. The upshot of all of this regulation is that the prospective franchisee is provided with meaningful disclosure information about the franchise opportunity and with enhanced statutory protection against violators.

As may be expected, there are conflicts between the Revised Rule and the laws of the various registration states. The FTC resolved this matter by requiring the franchisor to abide by both laws by selecting that portion of the state or federal law that gives the franchisee the greatest protection and the most disclosure information.

In all cases then, the franchisor must draft a multi-part disclosure document called the franchise disclosure document (FDD), which may range in size from 50 pages to several hundred pages. Once completed, the FDD is given to the prospective franchisee (that means you), who is then given a *minimum* of 14 calendar days within which to review the entire FDD. We talk more about this later in this chapter.

ANATOMY OF THE FDD

The first section of the FDD is the disclosure portion. In this part, the franchisor is required to respond to specific questions that are collected under 23 Items, each with a mandated title. The 23 Items cover various topics and covenants that are found in the franchise agreement. The FDD booklet is *not* a contract between the franchisor and you. Instead, it collects in one place all information that the FTC believes is relevant for the franchisee to have before making the purchase decision. The only contract between the franchisor and you is the franchise agreement and other contracts secondary to the franchise agreement. We talk more about the franchise agreement later in this chapter.

The second section contains the various exhibits required under the Revised Rule. In those exhibits, the franchisor is required to: (i) provide an exact copy of the franchise agreement and all contracts between franchisor and franchisee that the franchisee is expected to sign; (ii) deliver a list of state agencies that regulate franchising or that are serving as a registered agent for the franchisor; (iii) provide the franchisor's most recent financial statements, which in most cases must be audited under United States generally accepted accounting and auditing procedures; (iv) deliver the names, addresses, and other contact information of all of the current franchisees and the same information for all franchisees that left the franchise system during the most recently completed fiscal year; (v) the names and contact information of any trademark-specific franchisee associations; (vi) the table of contents of the operations manuals that are given to the franchisee by the franchisor; and (vii) the "receipt." The companion website (www.franchisebiblestudy.com) shows a complete FDD and includes the complete FTC Revised Rule.

The physical format of the document is highly formalized and requires: (i) an FTC-required cover page with specific language and disclosures; (ii) a "State Cover Page" drafted by the North American Securities Administrators Association (NASAA), which again, contains specific information including "risk factors;" (iii) the table of contents; and (iv) the information as organized by the Items.

The FTC looked to the NASAA to devise a complete set of compliance rules for the Revised Rule. These rules are collected in the NASAA 2008 Franchise Registration and Disclosure Guidelines. We have included the entire document on www.entrepreneur.com/franchiseresources.

THE COVER PAGES AND TABLE OF CONTENTS

The FTC and the NASAA require that every FDD in the United States start with two cover pages. The first is mandated by the FTC, and the second, titled "State Cover Page," is required through the NASAA Guidelines.

The Franchise Disclosure Document includes the language that *must* be included in each cover page. The franchisor cannot deviate from this language. The State Cover Page contains "Risk Factors." Again, the language of each of the three risk factors is mandatory. In reviewing FDDs, however, you may see that there are more than three risk factors. That usually means that a registration state has required the franchisor to include additional risk factors in order to register. The Revised Rule allows this to happen, and it is in this way that the franchisor is then required to provide you with the greatest disclosure and the most protection.

The NASAA State Cover Page includes a page called the "State Effective Dates." In the registration states, the franchisor is not allowed to offer a franchise until it has been registered—and is thus "effective." This page will list the date that each registration state has approved the FDD for sale. If you are in a registration state, take a look at this page to find out if: (i) your franchisor is registered in your state; and (ii) whether you were given the FDD after that date. A violation of either of those requirements means that the franchisor has broken the law.

The table of contents simply lists the correct title of each Item and points you to the page where it can be found.

THE ITEMS

The heart and soul of the disclosure portion and indeed its very purpose is set forth in the Items. As previously noted, each Item is given a specific title (which cannot be altered), and within each Item, the franchisor is required to provide the answers to a myriad of FTC-mandated questions. Once again, take a look at the NASAA Guidelines on the companion website (www.franchisebiblestudy.com) for a complete list of the questions in each Item.

The following sections specify the list of Items (by correct title) along with a description of the content to be found there.

Item 1. The Franchisor, and any Parents, Predecessors, and Affiliates

Item 1 gives you the franchisor's background and that of any parent company, predecessors, and affiliates. A *predecessor* is defined as "a person from whom the franchisor acquired directly or indirectly the major portion of its assets." An *affiliate* is defined as "a person controlled by, controlling, or under common control with the franchisor."

Examine this Item closely. Read about the background of the business and the business experiences of its principal officers. If possible, run a credit check on the company and its previous officers. In addition, any information you can obtain regarding the record of the previous businesses—including other franchise businesses in which the principals were associated—is of paramount importance. This information can also help you make some type of forecast about the possibility of your own success.

Item 2. Business Experience

This Item gives you the past five years' worth of the personal business experience of the franchisor's directors, trustees, general partners, officers, and any other individuals who will have management responsibility relating to the offered franchises. Remember that these folks are the ones you will be working with during your entire franchise experience. They should have experience operating as a franchisor. You—the franchisee—are the "customer" of the franchisor and as such should be treated that way. The fact

You should make every attempt to get to know the people who make up the franchisor's team as much as you can *before* you sign the franchise agreement. All business relationships are part business and part social and psychological. If you don't like them as people, chances are you will not like them as franchisors. Ask to see the head person before you put your money down. Remember, this person will be a vital part of your story of success, since his or her endeavors will directly affect you.

that the personnel have loads of experience in operating the business that is the model of the franchise *does not* mean that they have the ability to operate the franchisor, which is a separate and distinct business from franchised business. It is often the case, especially with new franchises, that the personnel will have great experience operating the *franchised business* but will have little or no experience or expertise in operating the *franchisor business*.

Item 3. Litigation

This Item requires special scrutiny during the review process. The franchisor must disclose any material litigation involving the franchisor and predecessor, parent, and affiliate, if the litigation involves claims about the franchisor's sales process, their performance under the franchise documents, and claims of antitrust, fraud, unfair or deceptive trade practices, or comparable allegations. The Revised Rule now requires the franchisor to disclose any franchisor-initiated litigation against its franchisees and any other business litigation (even if it is not franchise-related) if, at the end of the day, the litigation negatively impacts the franchisor's financial condition or their ability to operate a franchise.

As you may imagine, a franchisor that is mired in litigation will be less attractive and may indeed be a franchisor to avoid. Although most mature franchisors will have some litigation history—more often than not started by a terminated franchisee, or started by the franchisor against a terminated franchisee—you should stay away from any franchisor that is under a current injunction or restrictive order, particularly one that could result in a drastic change in the franchise operation, such as termination of the franchise. In addition, determine whether or not the franchisor or any of the franchisor's key employees have been convicted of crimes or have a record of unfavorable determinations handed down by courts or government agencies.

Item 4. Bankruptcy

This Item must disclose any bankruptcy in the last ten years that involved the franchisor and any parent, predecessor, affiliate, officer, or general partner of the franchisor, or any other individual who will have management responsibility relating to the sale or operation of the franchise.

> If the FDD mentions any such investigations, convictions, or proceedings, view these as warning signs and rethink whether or not you want to purchase the franchise. If you still wish to purchase the franchise, at least check out the proceedings as documented in the courts or government agencies and determine what has taken place in regard to this litigation.

Many great people have incurred numerous failures in their lives before reaching a pinnacle of success. Abraham Lincoln, who failed in the operation of a general store and in his first election, is just one of many such examples.

But if the bankruptcy involves a related prior business of one of the principal people, then you may treat it as a warning sign that he or she may not have the business acumen needed to successfully operate the franchisor.

Item 5. Initial Fees

Here the franchisor (and any of their affiliates) must disclose all of the initial fees they charge to the franchisee before opening. Such fees include the initial fee paid to purchase the franchise rights (often called the "initial franchise fee" or IFF), computer or point-of-sale equipment that must be purchased only from franchisor or their affiliates, and similar fees. IFFs range from a few thousand dollars to over $70,000. The "normal" range is between $25,000 and $40,000. We emphasize the word "normal" because this is one of the fees that is sensitive in competition. If another franchisor in the same sector is charging $25,000 and the franchisor you are talking to is charging substantially less or more, then you should look to see what, if anything, supports the difference. If there is nothing, then it is one of those times that the lower price should win.

Beware also of franchisors that "nickel and dime" you. For instance, some franchisors charge an initial franchise fee that is lower than the competition—but then assess tuition (a "training fee") in order to attend their training. They may charge a fee to receive the operations manual, a fee for having one of their personnel visit your business to help with opening, and so on. Many times, these fees together with the IFF equal more than the competitor's higher IFF. From a marketing point of view, it seems more beneficial to charge a higher IFF (subject to market pressures) and then provide the other goods and services without charge.

Remember that a high initial franchise fee does not necessarily mean the franchise is a better investment or even a good one. Moreover, a low initial franchise fee is not necessarily an indication of a bad investment. Some of the most successful franchise operations have had low initial franchise fees.

Item 6. Other Fees

This section of the FDD advises you in a table of any other fees that you will have to pay to the franchisor or an affiliate as well as costs that are collected by the franchisor for third parties, or that are otherwise imposed. Line items include a statement of the royalties, advertising fees, service fees, training fees, renewal fees, and other similar one-time or ongoing charges. Check to see if the franchisor will refund these fees if you decide to back out after signing the franchise agreement.

Once again, the fees charged here should be in line with the fees charged by other franchisees in the same business sector. This is one of the times that the formatting required by the Revised Rule allows you to more easily compare one system to another. You should use these figures when drafting your business plan.

Almost all systems will charge a "royalty" and one or more "advertising" fees. The royalty and advertising fees are usually expressed as a flat fee or a percentage of the "gross sales," "gross revenue," "net sales," and similar titles. Our FDD on the companion website (www. franchisebiblestudy.com) shows a royalty that is *both* a flat fee and a percentage fee. Carefully review the definition of revenue that is used to calculate the percentage. This is one of those places where franchisors are free to define that revenue in any way they choose, such that the "gross sales" definition for one franchisor may be materially different than the definition of the same term in another FDD.

> Check with your accountant to find out if the definition of revenue is reasonable.

Item 7. Estimated Initial Investment

Once again, using a table format, the franchisor must disclose a range of the minimum and maximum of all fees, costs, and expenses that the franchisee will incur prior to opening the business. This table will reflect the initial franchise fee, real property expenses such as rent and construction costs, the cost for computer equipment and similar line items. As with Item 6, the formatting of this important item allows you to easily compare the cost-to-open bottom line of one franchise opportunity to that of any other franchise opportunity. Competitive pressures should apply to the bottom line, meaning that the franchisors in the same business sector should charge similar fees.

The expenses here must include both pre-opening expenses and those incurred during the "initial phase," which is at least three months or a reasonable period for the industry. Along with Item 6, the information outlined here is extremely useful in mapping your business plan and your budget. Again, if at all possible, contact current franchisees and see if these cost projections appear fairly accurate according to their experience. If there are no current franchisees, review these listed costs with local contractors and vendors. Also remember that if these figures are materially misrepresented—that is, if you end up paying 50 percent more than is stated—it may be a violation of the law.

Item 8. Restrictions on Sources of Products and Services

It is a hallmark of franchising that the franchisor requires the franchisees to buy the goods and service needed to open only from approved vendors. It is the way that the franchisor can be assured of uniformity. For instance, it is typical for a franchisor to require the franchisee to purchase electronic equipment, food products, and similar goods and services only from sources approved in advance.

> If possible, check with current franchisees to see how they feel about any purchase restrictions and whether or not they are receiving their money's worth.

Item 8 also calls out the franchisor's specifications for permitting a new vendor into the system, and will identify any revenue that the franchisor receives from the required purchases, including rebates received by the franchisor from any supplier.

Item 9. Franchisee's Obligations

This Item consists of a table listing your obligations as a franchisee, with references to the sections of your franchise agreement that contain the obligations. The purpose of the table is to identify your principal obligations under the franchise agreement and other agreements. The table should help you find more detailed information about your obligations in these agreements and in other Items of the FDD.

Item 10. Financing

It continues to be true that obtaining financing to help purchase a franchise is still a challenge. Though it would be logical for the franchisor to sponsor financing, the fact is that very few franchisors make such an offer. In the case where financing is offered, usually it is for only a portion of the

Item 7 expenses. For instance, the franchisor may offer to finance the IFF or the computer system needed for operation, but will not finance the entire cost to open the business. If the franchisor offers financing, it must disclose in this Item the terms of such financing, including the amount it will agree to finance, the interest rate, and the length of the loan, and must also disclose the consequences for failing to pay, which often is the termination of the franchise agreement along with the statement that franchisor will sue to get payment.

> Contact your local bank to see if it will finance you. Also talk with the Small Business Administration, which can give you a list of local banks that offer SBA guaranties. If financing is offered by the franchisor, contact current franchisees to see what you can find out from them about their experiences with financing from the franchisor. Common sense is a requirement for all potential franchisees when investing hard-earned money in a franchise.

The ability to afford the purchase while still maintaining your lifestyle must be one of the criteria you use when making the "buy/don't buy" business decision.

Item 11. Franchisor's Assistance, Advertising, Computer Systems, and Training

This is one of the more lengthy and important disclosure Items. Though the instructions for this Item go on for pages, we will discuss here the most important matters that must be disclosed.

Here the franchisor must disclose the services they will provide to the franchisee before and after opening. These services are often stated as a list. Do not be surprised if the list is not long. That is usual in franchising. What you care about is whether the services that are offered are sufficient to help you open and then build the business. Talking with current franchisees about this is a very important part of your due diligence.

Additionally, this Item will describe all advertising expenditures you are expected to assume. Most often franchisors will require you to spend a certain dollar amount or percentage of your gross sales on local advertising. These figures can range from $150 to $2,000 or more each month, with the percentage ranging from 1 to 5 percent.

> Money spent on local advertising is the best investment you can make to attract customers.

Another advertising expenditure might be a fee (again expressed as a flat fee or percentage and paid to the franchisor) for national advertising. Unless the franchisor is a mature system with a significant number of franchisees (50 or more), money delivered to the franchisor for national advertising generally does franchisees little good. It is often used to create national advertising campaigns and the like, which may or may not air in your locale. Sometimes the money is used to generate advertising copy for use by franchisees, but it is then the franchisee's burden to pay for the placement of such advertising. Other advertising expenditures may include mandatory participation with neighboring franchisees in an advertising cooperative and may include advertising for a grand opening event.

This Item also calls for the franchisor to disclose the average time it takes a franchisee to open. This is measured from the date that the franchisee signs the franchise agreement to the date that he or she opens. For brick-and-mortar operations, this could range between four months and one year. For non-brick-and-mortar operations, the range of time could be as little as a few weeks to just a few months.

The franchisor is required to state the type of computer and similar electronics necessary to operate the business. As most businesses today operate with computers and through the internet, this disclosure takes on special importance.

Next, the franchisor must also give you a detailed description of the training you can expect to receive. Adequate training is another hallmark of a good franchisor. Most franchisees will be new to the business that was bought and will be new to the role as "boss." The goal of the training should be to take you through all aspects of the delivery of the goods and services to the end users and should cover all of the basics—from bookkeeping to inventory management—of administering the business. Talking with current franchisees about the value of the training is a vital part of your due diligence. If the training is inadequate, or is done in an amateurish way, it is fair to be concerned about the franchisor's ability to help build a vibrant system.

This Item will also disclose the table of contents of the operations manuals. As with the training, the manuals should contain meaningful information on each part of the franchised business and should be done in a professional manner. If the table of contents is skimpy or is poorly drafted, it is fair to be concerned about the franchisor's ability to operate a good system.

If the business is at all site-specific (as would be a brick-and-mortar business), then the franchisor should supply site-selection support. Most franchisors offer such services, though it will always be the franchisee's responsibility to hire professionals of his or her own choosing and at his or her expense to help with the site selection process.

> Every franchisee went through the same things that you are going through. A telephone call to a franchisee might give you an opportunity to meet the owner and discuss matters. Perhaps an offer of lunch would help ensure his or her cooperation.

Item 12. Territory

The franchisor must disclose whether it offers the franchisee an "exclusive territory" within which to operate the business. An *exclusive territory* (sometimes called a *protected territory*) is a franchise term-of-art that means that the franchisor offers an area of protection around your business in which you will be the only business selling the franchised goods and services. With an exclusive territory, the franchisor is promising that it will not permit another franchisee to locate within the territory and that it will also refrain from putting a company-owned or affiliate-owned business there.

If an exclusive territory is *not* offered, the franchisor must include the following FTC-mandated disclaimer statement: *"You will not receive an exclusive territory. You may face competition from other franchisees, from outlets that we own, or from other channels of distribution or competitive brands that we control."* Franchisors in the same business sector may or may not offer exclusive territories; and there is no right or wrong answer to this. It would seem that it would be in your best interest to always have an exclusive territory. The fact is, however, that franchised businesses with and without exclusive territories enjoy the same level of success. But if one of the reasons you want to buy a business is to have an exclusive territory, then this is the place where you find that answer.

This Item must also disclose whether you can relocate, and if so, what the criteria are for your move and whether you have any rights to purchase additional units.

One of the more important disclosures is whether you are required to meet a quota or perform in some other manner as a way of insuring either your right to an exclusive territory, or your right to continue in business at all. Once again, franchisors are all over the board on this: Some require it, while others don't. Quotas can be seen as a good way to insure that the system will contain motivated franchisees that are willing to work to make the quotas. On the other hand, quotas can be seen as an artificial way to measure the success (or failure) of each franchisee and as a method to place undue pressure on the franchisee. If a quota is required, it is important to talk with current franchisees about his or her experience with quota. Find out if the quotas are realistic. If the quota is too low, it loses its value as a motivational tool. If it is too high, then

> If an exclusive territory is not offered, find out whether the franchisor will give you a "right of first refusal" so you can purchase any additional franchises that may be offered in the future adjacent to your specified territory or location. This way, you will at least have the opportunity to avoid undue competition through your purchase of the territory in question.

the franchisor is setting up the franchisee for failure. Ask also about whether meeting the quota generates sufficient revenue to allow the franchisee to earn a reasonable living and to allow the franchisee to have a reasonable lifestyle. If quotas are very low, the mere fact that you have reached the quota does not insure that you are making a living from operating the business. On the other hand, if the quota is too high, you may earn a great living, but have little free time to enjoy it.

The information in this Item will also disclose the franchisor's reservation to itself of certain marketing and sales rights either within or outside any territory.

Item 13. Trademarks

One of the prime benefits you are paying for when you purchase a franchise is a well-known trade name, trademark, service mark, service name, or logotype (together known as the "Marks"). The FDD must identify each principal Mark to be licensed to you, and must state the franchisee's rights whether the franchisee is required to modify or discontinue use of a mark under any circumstances.

Preferably, you want to be a licensee of a Mark that is registered in the Principal Register of the U.S. Patent and Trademark Office (USPTO). There are two registers in existence: the Principal Register and the Supplemental Register. The Principal Register gives the franchisor the greatest protection against infringing users, which, in turn, gives the franchisee the right to use a Mark that has the best chance of always being around. If the Mark is registered with the USPTO, this Item requires the franchisor to disclose the registration number, the date that it was registered, and other information. Go online to the USPTO website (www.uspto.gov) and read about how you can search for the Mark. Sad though it may be, some franchisors claim to be registered but are not. This easy due diligence will help you make that determination. This Item may also disclose that the franchisor has applied for registration but has not yet received it. The fact that the franchisor has not yet received registration does not mean that it won't get registration. It means only that a final decision has not been made. If, however, the Mark is not allowed to be registered, then the franchisor (and franchisee) are left to decide on whether to get a new Mark. If a new Mark is chosen, this Item will tell you whether the franchisor or you will pay the cost necessary to change your printed materials and signage.

Once the Mark is registered, then and only then can the franchisor advertise using the ® symbol.

Registration of a trademark is only one element to consider. Here are some other questions to address:

- Are the Marks well known in the market area in which you intend to operate?
- Is the Mark so identified with the goods and services offered that merely seeing the Mark informs the public of the goods and services sold thereby attracting customers to the franchise operations?

Item 14. Patents, Copyrights, and Proprietary Information

The section on patents and copyrights is important to you only if patents are material to the franchise. If so, obtain copies of the patents from the U.S. Patent Office and have your patent attorney review them for depth of coverage and length of time remaining on the patent. Determine whether there are any possible limitations of the right of the franchisor to use the patent or any dissolution of the patent through licenses to others, particularly potential competitors. Carefully examine any claims of proprietary right and confidential information designated by the franchisor.

Most franchisors will also claim common-law copyright protection for all of their printed materials, including the franchise agreement and manuals.

Item 15. Obligation to Participate in the Actual Operation of the Franchise Business

This section discloses whether the franchisee must personally participate in the operation of the franchise. If there is no such requirement, this section must state whether the franchisor recommends such participation, whether the person that is handling day-to-day operations must complete the franchisor's training program, and whether this person must own an equity interest in the franchisee entity.

In the opinion of most franchise professionals, the successful franchisee is the one who manages their own business or at least spends considerable time supervising the management of the business. The smart franchisor, in many cases, will insist that the franchisee be active in the operation of the business or at least retain qualified managers who will be active.

Item 16. Restrictions on What the Franchisee May Sell

In most cases, the franchisor will require the franchisee to sell only the goods and services that are part of the franchised business. For instance, a pizza franchisor will not want its franchisees selling hot dogs, and will not want the franchisee to offer home-cleaning services in the same business. That is only logical.

There have been instances in which franchisees were limited to only one service. In one case, for example, a franchisee was limited to offering only oil-change service for automobiles. Franchisees of the system thought that the system should also offer general vehicle repair services since the oil-change business was not bringing in sufficient revenue. The question to ask yourself is whether or not such restrictions on your product sales will permit you to make a reasonable profit.

Item 17. Renewal, Termination, Transfer, and Dispute Resolution

Item 17 contains a cross-referencing table to the franchise agreement for 23 separate line items. It is different than Item 9 in that it includes a concise statement of the content of the particular franchise-agreement covenant as well as the location of the covenant in the agreement.

Pay attention to the "term" (length) of the Franchise Agreement (Item 17 (a)), the renewal provisions (Items 17 (b) and (c)), the termination covenants (Items 17 (c) through (i)), your rights to transfer the franchise (Items 17 (j) through (o)), the consequences of the franchisee's death or disability (Item 17 (p)), the non-competition covenants (Item 17 (r)), and the dispute-resolution covenants found at Items 17 (u) through (w).

If your registration state has franchise laws regulating franchise renewals and terminations, consult your attorney to see if the FDD's renewal and termination clauses comply with them. Go to the companion website (www.franchisebiblestudy.com) for more information on individual state franchise laws.

A good franchise package should definitely allow you to change legal forms of business organization—for example, from a sole proprietorship to a partnership, or from a sole proprietorship or partnership to a corporation or limited liability business entity—at a minimum fee.

Item 18. Public Figures

This section requires the franchisor to disclose whether it uses a famous person to endorse the franchise. If so, it must disclose the compensation paid or promised to the person, the person's involvement in management or control of the franchisor, and the amount of the person's investment in the franchisor. If the franchisor is paying a public figure to endorse the franchise, find out whether or not you can use the person in personal appearances or in advertising without prior written approval of the franchisor, how frequently you can do so, and the cost of such use, if any.

Item 19. Financial Performance Representations

According to the Revised Rule, a Financial Performance Representation (FPR) is:

"Any representation, including any oral, written, or visual representation, to a prospective franchisee, including a representation in the general media that states, expressly or by implication, a specific level or range of actual or potential sales, income, gross profits, or net profits." In layperson's terms, this refers to any document, chart, arithmetic calculation, math formula, or other representation that would allow a potential to determine what he or she could earn. For instance, the franchise seller that tells you that "you will easily earn $10,000 a month once you are open" is such a representation. The only way the franchisor or its sales staff or brokers can offer an FPR is if it is stated in this Item 19. So using our example, if the franchisor has written evidence that "x percent" of its total number of franchisees "earned" $10,000 a month within y months of opening, then the salesperson is being accurate. If no such information is found in Item 19, any claims made by the franchisor as to your potential earnings is in violation of the law. This does *not* mean that the franchisees are prohibited from telling you this information. In fact, they are the very best source to get exactly this information. It is only the franchisor that is prohibited from making any kind of FPR, unless it is stated in Item 19.

Most franchisors do not make FPRs, and the reason is simple: They want to avoid litigation. If the franchisor makes a legitimate FPR, and then a franchisee fails to meet that level of performance, and even though any FPR is accompanied by disclaimers that say in essence, "you cannot expect to make this much," the franchisee's failure to meet the level of performance is often the reason for litigation between the franchisor and franchisee.

If, however, the franchisor does provide such information, you should show it to your accountant for evaluation. This information should also be evaluated against any information that may be supplied by the franchisees and even by competitive franchise systems. If it is not possible for you to contact a franchisee of either the franchisor or a competitor, a suitable alternative would be to contact someone who is not a franchisee but operates a similar business in the same geographical area. This applies to your efforts to ferret out any of the information described earlier. There is nothing like relying on experience when deciding whether or not to buy a business.

If the franchisor does not make an FPR, the FDD will include a statement to that effect. It will also state that no employee or representative is authorized by the franchisor to make such representations.

Item 20. Outlets and Franchise Information

This section of the disclosure document provides, in tabular form, information regarding existing outlets in the franchise system. It covers outlet transfers—and the status of franchised and company-owned outlets—for the last three fiscal years, as well as projected openings for the next fiscal year. It must also provide information regarding any reporting changes, any confidentiality clauses signed by franchisees during the last three fiscal years ("gag clauses"), and information about certain trademark franchisee associations.

> Generally, the more franchisees, the greater the franchisor's chances for success in future sales of franchises; however, don't take this at face value. Check with the franchisees themselves. Theoretically, a higher number of franchisees indicate a more extensive distribution of the product and a better public image for the franchise.

In addition to accessing information about existing outlets, you can also determine whether a substantial number of failures have occurred within the franchised operation you are investigating. You can also project just how large the system probably will be in a few years, according to the estimates of the franchisor.

Item 21. Financial Statements

The FDD must contain an exhibit with the franchisor's audited financial statements for the prior three fiscal years. If the franchisee has been open less than three years, the FTC allows the franchisor to phase in audits. This is not always the case for the registration states, though. For example, Hawaii requires audited financials even for a startup franchisor.

Take the financial statements to your accountant if you do not have the training to properly evaluate them. Remember that the financial condition of the franchisor not only will affect his or her ability to run a financially successful operation in the future, but it will also determine whether or not he or she will go under, leaving you holding the bag. Most good franchisors have one or more of their own successful company-owned units, which units formed the basis of their franchise systems. Feel free to ask questions of the main representatives of the franchisor concerning these financial statements.

Most franchisors use a separate corporate entity for selling their franchises. However, if your particular franchisor doesn't, you then have an opportunity to find out whether or not these company-owned ventures actually made any income for a period of up to three years. If the franchisor can't make a go of the business, how do you expect to do so?

The franchisor is also required in section 21 to provide a separate, audited financial statement for a company controlling 80 percent or more of the franchisor. An affiliate's audited financial statement may be used in lieu of the franchisor's financial statement if the affiliate guarantees performance.

Item 22. Contracts

This section requires the franchisor to attach to the FDD a copy of all form contracts the franchisee will sign, including the franchise agreement, leases, options, and purchase agreements.

Item 23. Receipt

In this final section, the franchisor is required to include as the last page of the FDD a form for the prospective franchisee to sign to acknowledge receipt of the FDD.

THE ANATOMY OF THE FRANCHISE AGREEMENT

The franchise agreement is the contract between the franchisor and you. The 23 Items listed in the preceding section must accurately reflect the content of the franchise agreement. If the language of the franchise agreement differs from what is stated in the 23 Items, there is a problem. A simple rule of thumb for differentiating the sections of the FDD from that of the franchise agreement is the way in which the sections are labeled. The FDD sections are called Items (i.e., Item 1 through 23). The sections of the franchise agreement are called Articles.

The franchise agreement is not a "standard" or "form" agreement. The format of the contract differs from one franchise system to another. Some agreements are as small as a few dozen pages; others can run 70 pages or more. Each one, however, will have all of the information disclosed in Items 5 and 6, and Items 8 through 18 of the FDD within the corresponding Articles of the agreement. For instance, Item 5 tells us what you will pay directly to the franchisor (or its affiliate) before you open. Remembering that the FDD Items are *not* a contract, in order for the franchisor to get paid, it must include these fees in the body of the franchise agreement. Item 6 describes what additional fees or expenses you have to pay the franchisor during the operation of the franchised business, and, again, the obligation to make such payments must be included in the franchise agreement if the franchisor wants to collect. Items 1 through 4 are not reflected in the franchise agreement because they contain general information about the franchisor that need not be repeated. Item 7 tells you what you can expect to pay to open your unit. Again, the franchise agreement will not repeat this table, though it will state that you have to incur expenses for all of the line items identified in the Item. Items 20 through 23 are likewise not repeated since they are general information about the franchisor.

Absent taking a 20-hour law school class on the specifics of any one franchise contract, there is no practical way to go over every conceivable covenant that could be in a franchise agreement. But this is where an *experienced franchise lawyer* comes into play. In the same way that doctors have specialties (you would not go to a cardiologist to have your brain examined), lawyers are also specialized, with franchise law being one such group. Your family lawyer, the lawyer you used to set up your business entity, and your estate lawyer are all specialized in those areas. Unless the attorney has significant experience in franchise law, however, he or she will be doing you a disservice by representing you in the franchise-law setting.

Though each franchise agreement will differ in style, language, and content, all franchise agreements have covenants that address special areas of the franchise relationship. We will briefly review those. Once again, the franchise agreement on the companion website (www.franchisebiblestudy.com) will have the specific language that addresses each covenant. Though we have grouped them in the same way as the franchise agreementon the website, franchisors are not bound by law to have any special sequence of covenants.

The Covenants

The franchise agreement is a contract. Contracts contain any number of covenants, each of which describes a promise, right, or duty that the franchisee or franchisor owes to the other or that benefits the franchisor or franchisee. Though each franchisor changes the order in which it puts the covenants, and remembering that no franchise agreement contains exactly the same covenants, the following is a list of those covenants that one most often sees in a typical franchise agreement.

Grant of Franchise

The franchise agreement contains trademark-licensing language. The "Grant" section lets the franchisee know that the franchisor is granting him or her the limited, non-transferable, non-exclusive right to use the franchisor's trademarks, logos, services marks (called generally the Marks), and the franchisor's system of operation (often called the System) for the period of time defined by the franchise agreement. The franchisee receives no ownership rights to the Marks or the System, and the franchisor always retains the right to terminate the franchisee's grant-of-license because of a breach of the franchise agreement.

Opening Date, Territory Limitations, Build-Out, and Similar Rights

This covenant will repeat language from Items 11 and 12. It will describe the franchisee's territory (be it exclusive or not) and set up a time schedule by which the franchisee must find a brick and mortar location, must have the plans for the unit approved and must be built-out and opened. This section may also disclose other matters such as the computer equipment needed to operate the business and the like.

If the franchise opportunity does not include the need for a brick and mortar, this section will be much shorter and will usually identify the territory and the requirements that the franchisee must meet in order to open the doors.

Fees and Required Purchases

This section will disclose the fees that are more specifically described in Items 5, 6, 7, 8, and 11. The fees include the initial franchise fee, any fees paid to the franchisor prior to opening, any fees paid to the franchisor during the term of the franchise, all advertising fee obligations, and the like. Some franchise agreements spread the fees over several sections of the franchise agreement. But if a fee stated in one of the Items is not identified in the franchise agreement, then the franchisor may be out of luck in trying to later claim the fee is due.

As noted in Items 8 and 11, most franchisors require the franchisee to purchase the goods and services needed to operate the franchised business only from vendors approved by the franchisor, or only through the franchisor or its affiliates. These covenants will describe those required purchases.

If the franchisor offers financing, it will be stated in this or in a similar covenant.

Advertising

Advertising (discussed in Item 11), is one of the pillars of a successful franchise operation. In this section the franchisor should repeat the franchisee's advertising obligations as they are stated in Item 11 (and the fees for which are identified in Items 5, 6, 7, 8, and 11—as applicable).

Term and Renewal

As mentioned, the *term* of the franchise agreement is the length of time measured from the date the franchise agreement is signed to the date that the franchise agreement expires. If the franchise relationship lasts for five years, the term is five years. (See Item 17 (a)). The term can be ended sooner if the franchisee breaches the agreement and the franchisor terminates the relationship.

The franchisor can offer no renewal, in which case the franchise agreement terminates on the last day of the initial term, or the renewal term, sometimes called the *successor term*, can be perpetual—meaning literally that the relationship can go on forever assuming the franchise relationship is not terminated because of the franchisee's breach—or it can continue for a limited number of extra years. Where the initial term is ten years, one often sees renewals being granted for one additional ten-year term, or for two or more five-year terms. A synopsis of the renewal covenants (and the location of the covenant in the franchise agreement) can be found in the Item 17 table in subsections (b) and (c).

If renewal rights are granted, this section will also state what prerequisites must be met in order to renew. It is usual to see a list that contains at least some of the following:

- The franchisee cannot be in breach of the franchise agreement on the date that he or she exercises the renewal right.
- The franchisee cannot have breached and then cured the breach of the franchise agreement more than x times (for example, three times) during the prior term.
- The franchisee will be required to pay a renewal fee (see Item 6).
- The franchisee is required to sign the then-current franchise agreement (which means that the terms of the new franchise agreement may be significantly different than those of the current franchise agreement).
- The franchisee may be required to update the brick-and-mortar location to the then-current standards.

In some cases, the franchisor will retain the right to refuse to grant a renewal even though the franchisee has met the requirements.

Services Offered by Franchisor

Though not all franchisors will repeat the Item 11 pre-opening and post-opening services that they offer the franchisee, sound drafting principals will require that these matters be repeated in the franchise agreement. In this way, there is a clear contractual obligation on the part of the franchisor to deliver the services it has promised in Item 11. Even if the franchisor does not include the statement of services, the Revised Rule states that the franchisor cannot make a promise in the disclosure and then later disclaim the promise in the franchise agreement, meaning that if push was to come to shove, the franchisee could try to enforce the Item 11 statements. Including them in the franchise agreement, however, removes the specter of litigation as a way to insert rights into the contract that are not otherwise stated.

Protection of Proprietary Information, Marks, and Other Intellectual Property

As discussed in the "Grant of Franchise" section earlier, the franchisor is granting only a temporary license to the franchisee. Most franchisors will enforce this understanding by adding specific language that identifies each item that makes up its proprietary, confidential, and trade-secret information and by then stating the limitations that are placed on the franchisee's right to use such information. It is important protection for the franchisor and is not usually a covenant missing from the franchise agreement.

Training

Somewhere in the franchise agreement, the franchisor must state that they will provide training. This section of the franchise agreement may be a repetition of the language in Item 11, though it is more usual to see language that states simply that the franchisor will provide training. This section should also disclose any additional training, seminars, meetings, or the like that the franchisor will either require or will urge the franchisee to attend.

Quality Control

As the name suggests, franchisors will address the franchisee's specific quality-control requirements. This is sound franchising and is necessary to insure that the goods and services offered throughout the system meet the franchisor's minimum requirements.

Transfers

Virtually all franchise agreements control the franchisee's right to transfer their interest in the franchise relationship. As with the renewal, the franchisor will determine whether to grant the transfer. It is usual to see the following in the list of transfer prerequisites:

- The franchisee cannot be in breach of the franchise agreement on the date that he or she exercises the renewal right.
- The franchisee cannot have breached and then cured the breach of the franchise agreement more than x times (for example, three times) during the prior term.
- The franchisor will determine whether the transferee meets the then-current qualifications imposed on new franchisees.
- The franchisee or transferee will be required to pay the transfer fee (see Item 6).
- The transferee will be required to sign the then-current franchise agreement (which means that the terms of the new franchise agreement may be significantly different than those of the current franchise agreement).
- The transferee will be required to complete all training.
- The transferee may be required to update the brick and mortar location to the then-current standards.

Defaults, Damages, and Complaint Limitations

All franchise agreements will contain some recitation of the violations of the franchise agreement that will be treated as a breach. These violations may be divided into those breaches that result in the immediate termination of the franchise agreement, for which no cure is given, and those violations for which cure is provided.

Most often the breaches for which no cure is given include the following:

- Abandonment of the business can mean a period as short as a few days to as long as 14 days. *Abandonment* means that you have either intentionally closed the business for good or have be forced to close for some other reason—even a death in the family. The franchisor reasonably expects the franchisee to have a contingency plan that allows the business to continue, even in the face of an unexpected problem.

- Insolvency of the franchisee, bankruptcy of the franchisee, or similar occurrences, which point to the franchisee's inability to finance the business.

- Intentional or negligent misuse of the Marks or other intellectual property belonging to the franchisor.

- Material violation of certain laws, including criminal laws, that results in damage to the good will of the franchised business.

- The breach of the franchise agreement (each of which breach was cured—if cure was even offered) more than *x* times during the prior term. This may be as few as one or two to sometimes four or more.

- The failure to pay taxes or employees.

It is usual for the franchise agreement to state something to the effect that the franchisee will be given between five and 30 days to cure any other breach of the franchise agreement not otherwise listed in the "no-cure" list.

It is also usual for the franchise agreement to contain a so-called *cross-default* provision. This covenant states that the franchise agreement can be terminated (even if its terms were not breached) if the franchisee breaches and fails to cure some other agreement — be it a different franchise agreement with the franchisor, the loss of the lease for a brick-and-mortar establishment, or another contract the termination of which would result in a material loss to the franchisee's ability to operate the business.

When the franchise is terminated because of an uncured (or incurable) violation, the franchisor has the right to ask for damages against the franchisee. These damages can be stated in the franchise agreement as a fixed dollar amount—called a *liquidated damages* covenant—or can be as general as a statement that the franchisor will have the right to seek any damages that it can prove it lost as a result of the franchisee's breach of the franchise contract. Included in this litany of damages will often be a statement that the franchisor has the right to seek damages measured by the loss of royalty payments that it otherwise would have enjoyed had the franchisee not breached the contract. Though this may sometimes be difficult to prove, franchisors have nonetheless been successful in getting these types of damages.

Many franchise agreements will also state that in the event of a violation of the franchise agreement by either party, the injured party must bring an action for relief within a stated period of time, which usually is one year from the date of the breach. This requires each party to be vigilant in its monitoring of the performance of the other party.

It is also usual for the franchisor to give themselves a greater period of time to cure any of its breaches than it gives the franchisee.

Obligations Upon Expiration or Termination

Once the franchise relationship has ended—either because the term has naturally concluded and no renewal has occurred, or because the franchise agreement was terminated—it is usual for the contract to list a series of steps that the franchisee must take to "de-identify" the business and the franchisee's association with the franchise system. These often include the following:

- Remove all external and interior signage.
- Destroy all letterhead, business cards, and any other printed material that bears the franchisor's Mark or other intellectual property.

- Return to the franchisor all operations manuals.
- Terminate any websites, email addresses, telephone numbers, or the like that may be associated with the franchised business. In this regard, it is also usual for the franchisor to require the franchisee to assign to the franchisor all such items and services with the understanding that the franchisor may use the same numbers and contact information to put a new franchisee into the old franchisee's territory or physical location.
- Terminate any leases—again with the caveat that many franchisors have in place an agreement with the landlord or other lessor that permits the franchisor to take physical possession of the real estate lease, equipment lease, or the like, so that the franchisor can immediately reopen either as a company-owned unit, or as a new franchisee's franchised business.
- Notify all suppliers, vendors, and the like that the franchisee is no longer associated with the franchised system.

Franchisor's Right of First Refusal

Most franchise agreements give the franchisor the option, but not the obligation, to exercise a first right refusal to purchase the franchisee's business—in the case where the franchisee seeks to transfer the business, or the first right to purchase the franchisee's assets at the time that the franchise agreement expires or is terminated. In the former case, the franchisor will usually agree to step into the shoes of the proposed transferee and will pay the franchisor the same amount as was promised by the proposed transferee. In the latter case, the franchisor will most often agree to pay the "fair market value."

Relationship Between the Parties

Franchisees are always treated as independent contractors of the franchisor (in legalese, sometimes called the *principal* in such a relationship). This has several important implications. An independent contractor is *not* an employee or agent of the principal. Instead, the independent contractor is in business for themselves. The parties to this relationship pay their own taxes, hire on their own, are responsible for their own employees, and generally operate independently of the other in carrying out the contract between them.

Recently, the independent contractor status between franchisor and franchisee has come under scrutiny by the U.S. Department of Labor. If in fact the franchisor-franchisee relationship is reclassified as that of employer (the franchisor) and employee (the franchisee), that would mean that the franchisee's employees would be "co-employed" by the franchisor, which would put a tremendous financial and compliance burden on the franchisor. Though no final decision on the federal level has been made as of the date of this edition, several states are considering legislation that would exempt the franchisor-franchisee relationship from the co-employment definition.

Indemnification

All franchisee agreements will contain an indemnification covenant. In the franchise setting, the *indemnification covenant* means that the franchisee will reimburse the franchisor for any losses it suffers as a result of some negligent act or wrongdoing of the franchisee. For example, if a customer of a franchisee were to slip and fall in the franchisee's store, the customer could sue the franchisee *and* the franchisor. In such a case, the franchisee would be responsible for all of the costs, fees (including attorneys' fees), and damages suffered by the franchisor as a result of being named in the lawsuit.

These covenants are almost always one-sided in favor of the franchisor—which is fair, given that the franchisee and not the franchisor is responsible for the day-to-day operation and maintenance of the business. In some cases, however, a franchisor may agree to indemnify the franchisee if the franchisor loses the right to use the Marks (perhaps because of a superior right to the Mark owned by a third party). There, the franchisor would agree to reimburse the franchisee for the cost of replacing signs, stationery, and other items carrying the franchisor's Marks.

Non-competition Covenant and Similar Restrictions

A *non-competition covenant* is one that seeks to prevent the franchisee from opening a business that would compete with the franchised business. Every state in the nation has some statute or case law that holds non-competition covenants to be unenforceable *unless* the relationship between the parties falls into one of the few exceptions. One of those exceptions is the franchisor-franchisee relationship. Even in that case, however, most states will only enforce such a covenant if, and only if, the definition of a "competitive business" is reasonable, the length of time during which the former franchisee is restrained from competing is reasonable, and the geographic territory of no competition is reasonable. On the other hand, California will not permit the enforcement of such a covenant because the legislature found it to be a restraint on the person's ability to make a living.

Virtually all franchise agreements will have non-competition covenants. The covenant is often broken into two parts: the "in-term" covenant; and the "post-term" covenant.

As the name suggests, the *in-term* covenant prevents the franchisee from competing against the franchisor and any other franchisees while the franchise agreement is in force. Typically this covenant covers a geographic area around each franchised, company-owned, and affiliate-owned business. Most states have enforced these covenants.

The *post-term* covenant covers the former franchisee after the franchise agreement expires or is earlier terminated because of an uncured breach. These covenants receive close scrutiny. The period of time that seems to be "reasonable" ranges from a few months up to five years. An acceptable geographic limitation depends on the type of business (a brick-and-mortar vs. a home-based operation), the goods and services offered (online vs. person to person), and similar factors. There is no particular range that can be identified.

Finally, the definition of a competitive business must be sufficiently similar to the franchised business to make it enforceable. Any one of the three variables may be unreasonable and may result in an unenforceable covenant. For instance, in the case of a pizza restaurant that also sells salads, calzones, and pasta dishes, a non-competition covenant that prevents the former franchisee from competing in a pizza restaurant (that may or may not sell salads, calzones, and pasta dishes) within five miles of any franchisee, company-owned, or affiliate-owned unit for a period of three years may be enforceable because each of the restrictions—the three years, five miles, and the identity of the competitive business being a pizza joint—is itself reasonable. On the other hand, if for instance only one of the variables were to change—such as changing the definition of a competitive business to "any restaurant"—the entire covenant could be thrown out, since "any restaurant" could include a hot dog stand that is no competition at all to a pizza place.

Recognizing that the determination of whether a covenant is enforceable is ultimately in the eye of the beholder, and given that these covenants in general are thought to be enforceable only in very limited circumstances, most franchise agreements contain a *savings covenant*—sometimes called a *blue pencil* rule (because judges used to mark up briefs using a blue pencil). This covenant gives the court or arbitrator the right to rewrite any offending limitation in order to make the covenant enforceable. In our case, then, the court could declare that the five-mile radius was fair, but that the three years should be reduced to one year and that the "any restaurant" definition be revised to "any restaurant that earns 30 percent or more of its revenue from the sale of pizzas."

Franchisors often try to include spouses, civil union partners, and even adult children of the franchisees in the scope of the non-competition covenants. In some cases, the courts have found in favor of this inclusion by reasoning that the family members are close enough that allowing competition by one of these members is the same as allowing the franchisee to compete. Other courts, though, have limited the scope of the covenant only to those persons who have signed the agreement.

Other restrictive covenants include clauses that prevent the solicitation of former employees and clauses that prevent the former franchisee from diverting business away from the franchise system. These covenants are not as closely reviewed, since they do not prevent the franchisee from earning a living but only seek to help the franchisor maintain a reasonable competitive edge.

Dispute Resolution

Several methods are used to resolve disputes between franchisor and franchisee. Most often one will see at least a nonbinding-mediation requirement followed by a binding-arbitration requirement. In other cases, these two methods of resolution will be preceded by the requirement that the parties first meet face-to-face.

All states favor the idea that court litigation be heard in its own state if the parties had sufficient contact with that state or if one of the parties started the litigation in the state. Thus, depending on who files first (the "plaintiff"), the franchisor or franchisee plaintiff will want the matter to be heard in their home state. In most registration states this choice is taken out of the hands of the litigants by statutory language that requires the matter to be heard in the franchisee's home state regardless of who starts the litigation. The federal courts, however, have determined that arbitration covenants—even ones that dictate the location of the arbitration (usually the franchisor's home state) and the choice of law to be used to interpret the dispute (usually being the law of the franchisor's home state)—will prevail over state law to the contrary. This gives the franchisor the distinct advantage of being able to call out their home state for each such purpose, while it burdens the franchisee with the requirement of hiring out-of-state legal counsel and with the requirement that the franchisee travel away from home. As a result, and in the "old days" (ten or so years ago) the requirement to go to court was dismissed in favor of arbitration. It was also thought that mediation and then arbitration was a faster and cheaper resolution method. In recent years however, arbitration has lost its swiftness, and the cost to litigate by this method has skyrocketed. Thus franchisors are at least revisiting the court alternative.

Insurance

All franchise agreements will require the franchisee to obtain insurance to cover its business operations. For the home-based business, the insurance may be minimal, whereas for the brick-and-mortar establishment, the insurance requirements will be substantial.

In all cases, each of the franchisee's insurance policies will require that the franchisor be named as an "additional insured," meaning that the franchisor enjoys the same coverage as does the franchisee, even though the franchisor is not paying for the coverage.

> Always have your insurance broker look at the insurance covenants to make sure that they are reasonable under the circumstances and have your broker give you quotes on the insurance premiums.

Additional or "Miscellaneous" Provisions

This is kind of the catch-all section of the franchise agreement that contains what some call "boilerplate" language, meaning that it is "usual" that such language be included in any contract. Although that may be true, each such covenant is no less important than any other covenant in the franchise contract; all things being equal, each covenant is enforceable. In virtually all franchise agreements, you will see the following covenants:

- *A "merger" covenant.* This is a statement to the effect that the entire agreement between the franchisor and franchisee is found within the four corners of the agreement itself and that all prior written agreements and oral statements are either included in the written franchise agreement (thus are "merged" into the contract), or if not included then they are not enforceable. Thus, if the franchisor has orally promised to pay for half of your build-out cost but has not reduced it to writing and made it part of the franchise agreement, then there is the strong likelihood that the statement would not be enforceable. It is for this reason that all franchisees should: (i) *read the whole franchise agreement*; and, (ii) reduce to writing and then incorporate into the franchise agreement any promises or statements made that the franchisee intends to rely upon during the franchise relationship.

- *A "modification" or "amendment" covenant.* This covenant simply confirms that once signed, the franchise agreement cannot be modified unless both parties agree in writing and that is signed and dated by franchisor and franchisee.

- *A "non-waiver" provision.* This covenant states that one or both of the parties will not be prevented from enforcing in the future a covenant in the franchise agreement simply because the party failed to enforce ("waived" enforcement) in the past.

- *A "notice" provision.* This provides for the manner and method by which the parties are to communicate with each other. It is usual for the parties to still communicate by snail mail for the most important matters (for example, notices of default), though many franchisors will accept email communication for less important matters.

- *An "invalidity" covenant.* This clause states that the fact that one or more covenants may be determined to be unenforceable will not prevent the balance of the contract from being enforceable.

- *A "time is of the essence" covenant.* This covenant states that each covenant must be timely performed. In other words, if the covenant requires performance in ten days, performance must be completed within the ten days.

- *A "survival" covenant.* In contract law, the enforcement of any covenant in a contract stops being enforceable on the date that the contract expires or is terminated unless there is language that states that certain covenants will continue to be enforceable (will "survive") even after that date. In the case of the franchise relationship, such surviving covenants include the non-competition clause, the prohibition from using the Marks or the intellectual property of the franchisor outside of the franchised business, and similar restrictive covenants.

- *A "guaranty" covenant.* A *guaranty* is used when the franchise is purchased through a business entity. In that case, the franchisor will want the owners of the business entity to personally guarantee that he or she will pay all fees and complete any performance that the franchisee fails to do. While this is usually the right-hand owners guaranteeing the performance of their left-hand business, it nonetheless legally binds the owners to perform and uses their personal assets as the collateral for such performance.
- *"Acknowledgement" covenants.* These covenants are included to insure that the franchise recognizes ("acknowledges") the risks involved in operating any business and to bring to the franchisee's attention that the franchisee has the right—and indeed should — consult with professionals of their choosing to insure that the franchise agreement and the entire franchise relationship are understood.
- *State-specific addenda.* Most registration states require the franchisor to build in a state-specific amendment to the franchise agreement in order to ensure that the particulars of its franchise law are known to the franchisee. If the franchisee is in a registration state, but no amendment or addendum is found, then it is worth calling your state to insure that the franchisor is in fact properly registered.

THE ANATOMY OF ATTACHMENTS TO THE FRANCHISE AGREEMENT

"Attachments," "Schedules," or "Exhibits" are found in most franchise agreements. These additional documents are important parts of the franchise agreement and are as enforceable as any covenant found in the body of the contract.

Though the types and content of these documents are as varied as the franchise systems themselves, one often finds the following:

- *Statement of Ownership.* This document requires the business entity franchisee to identify and then provide the contact information for each owner of the business and each of its executive or management personnel.

- *Description of the territory.* If it is not called out in the body of the franchise agreement, franchisors will identify the geographic limitations of the territory of the franchisee.

- *Credit/criminal background check consent.* More and more franchisors are requiring franchisees to submit to credit and criminal background checks. This can only be done with permission.

- *General Release.* As previously discussed, the general release is signed when the franchisor has granted the franchisee an additional right or privilege, including granting the right to renew or transfer. The General Release relieves the franchisor from liability for claims that may have arisen in the past.

- *Collateral Assignment of Lease.* This is completed between the franchisee and the landlord and is for the benefit of the franchisor. The assignment permits the franchisor to take over the franchisee's lease should the franchisee leave the premises because of expiration or earlier termination of the lease or the franchise agreement.

- *Collateral Assignment of Contact Information.* This is the form by which the franchisee grants the franchisor ownership of telephone numbers, email addresses, web addresses, and the like and is enforced upon the expiration or earlier termination of the franchise agreement.

- *State addenda.* See explanation in preceding section.

- *Guaranty.*

- *Closing Acknowledgement.* This document is used by the franchisor as a quiz of the franchisee and is used to insure that the franchisee has not been made promises that are outside of the franchise agreement's four corners, has not been denied the right to have professionals of its own choosing review the documents, and the like.

The decision to enter into the franchise relationship is no less important than the decision you make to purchase a home or to enter into any long-term relationship. It requires sober reflection on your needs and desires, on your abilities and limitations, and on your family, your health, and your financial and emotional well-being. You cannot and should not go it alone. Hire an experienced franchise attorney to help you better understand the documents and hire an accountant that has experience in franchising. Those relationships will be essential to your decision-making process.

Setting Up Your Business Entity

A franchise may be purchased by a natural person (often called a "sole proprietor") or by a business entity. In the United States, business entities include: general partnership; limited partnership; limited liability business entity (which includes a limited liability company, a limited liability partnership, and several other iterations and here called an LLC); or corporation.

The best advice that most franchise attorneys give their clients is to purchase the franchised business rights in the name of a business entity. But which one is best? The answer to this question is ultimately based on the situation of each franchisee and should be made by the franchisee's professional advisors (his or her franchise attorney and accountant), but the informed franchisee must first understand the risks and rewards of the various choices. This section will help you navigate these waters.

SOLE PROPRIETORSHIP AND GENERAL PARTNERSHIP

A *sole proprietorship*, as its name implies, is created by an individual who decides to open a business. Your child's lemonade stand is a sole proprietorship, as is your uncle's vacuum repair shop. Though the sole proprietorship requires no filings with the state before opening for business, and indeed is deemed to exist merely by the act of starting any kind of business and, by definition, is owned by one person, the sole proprietor is personally liable for all actions of the business, and his or her personal assets are subject to seizure by a creditor, the government, and third parties with whom the person has done business. The sole proprietor is taxed at his or her personal level, meaning that the profits and losses "pass through" for the benefit or burden of the individual. There is virtually no reason to elect to purchase the franchised business as a sole proprietor.

A general partnership is a step up from the sole proprietorship. A *general partnership* is defined as: (i) business entity; (ii) in which there are two or more "partners," each of whom shares: (a) equally in the management and daily operation of the business; (b) equally in the profits and losses; and, (c) equally in exposure to personal liability. Thus each partner can bind the business to legal obligations even when the other partner is unaware that the obligation was incurred. Some states require that the partnership file notice of the partnership, whereas others do not. Partnerships are taxed as a pass-through entity, meaning that the profits and losses flow directly to the partners without the need for the partnership entity itself to pay taxes. Once again, each partner's personal assets are exposed to the acts of each other partner.

> It is the specter of personal liability for the acts of the business that most often steers the knowledgeable franchisee away from electing the use of the sole proprietorship or general partnership. Instead, and as more fully discussed below, most franchisees in the know will choose a corporation or a limited liability business entity as the purchaser of the franchise.

CORPORATIONS AND LLCs

Most franchisees own the franchised business with other family members or with friends, and most have a very limited number of equity owners. Such business entities are said to be *closely held*, meaning that the business is owned and controlled by very few folks. This is important because it helps guide the entity choice. In most cases, because it is closely held, the owners will choose an S corporation or an LLC over any of the other options because these two entities offer significant tax benefits to the owners while also protecting the personal assets of the owners.

Corporations and LLCs are *not* designed or controlled by the federal government. Instead, each state has its own laws that define the setting up and then the operation of the business entity of choice. The federal government and the IRS have no input into this procedure. Assuming that the franchisee is not a publicly traded entity (which is the case in virtually all franchise relationships), the only time that the federal government "touches" the business entity is its taxation.

Corporations were originally created to provide their owners (the shareholders) a shield that protects their personal assets from the claims of the corporation's creditors and third parties. A *shareholder* of a corporation, be it a tiny corporation with one owner that does $1,000 of business a year or a behemoth that generates billions in revenue, cannot for the most part be made to pay a debt of the corporation, answer for the wrongdoing of the corporation, or be responsible for matters between the corporation and third parties. This protection is often called the *corporate shield* or *shield of protect*. Indeed, before the creation of the limited liability business entity, this shield of protection was unique to corporations (though some protection is offered to the limited partners of a limited partnership). Thus, general partnerships, joint ventures, the general partners in a limited partnership, and the like all more or less expose some or all of the owners to personal liability for the creditors of the entity.

The body of corporate business-entity law was handed down from the English and has for hundreds of years been interpreted first by English courts, and then by the courts of the United States. Due to this history, almost all states have the same basic rules, laws, and case law concerning corporations. This history has also informed our collective understanding of how a corporation works. Most of us know that a corporation has shareholders, a board of directors, and officers. We know that the business is controlled by bylaws that act as the roadmap for the operation of the business, and that the day-to-day operations of the business are controlled by the president, chief executive officer, vice president, treasurer, and secretary. As a society, we became comfortable with this general knowledge as it relates to the way the corporation is supposed to operate. Then came the limited liability business entity.

Unlike the corporation, the LLC concept is a creature of the United States that was conceived and formalized in 1977 by the state of Wyoming. A *limited liability business entity* (which includes the *limited liability company, limited liability general partnership, limited liability limited partnership,* and the like) is a non-corporate entity that is formed under the law of the state in which the entity is found for the purpose of protecting its owners from unlimited personal liability because of the acts of the business entity. Since 1977 all 50 states have passed LLC laws. As with corporations, the federal government has no say in the formation or operation of an LLC. It is only the taxation of the entity by the IRS that creates the nexus between the business entity and the federal government. The formation of the LLC, however, has been shrouded in mystery simply because it is the new kid on the block. We try to demystify it in this section.

If the owners of a corporation or an LLC all have protection from personal liability, then which business entity is right for the franchisee? For the most part, business folks in the United States have an innate sense of how a corporation works. For that reason, it is often chosen by default as the go-to business entity. Yet the upstart LLC has much to offer. To help make the final decision, let's look at the structure of each.

THE CORPORATION: BASIC STRUCTURE

The components of a corporation are: the shareholders (who "own" the business); the board of directors (the Board); the officers; and the employees. Under the law of most states, a corporation can have as few as one shareholder, meaning that from the point of view of protecting ones assets from claims, there is never a reason to be a sole proprietor.

The business course of the corporation is set when it is incorporated and the decision is made as to the purpose of the business. In our case, the purpose will be to own and successfully operate a franchised business. This is known as the *corporate purpose.*

Once the corporate purpose is set, it becomes the duty of the Board to do everything necessary to insure that the corporate purpose is met. Take note that the purpose of the Board is not to make money for the shareholders—though that of course is the ultimate hope and prayer—but is instead to steer the ship in such a way as to ensure that the corporate purpose is met.

The operations of the corporation are directed by a document called the bylaws. *Bylaws* are in essence the roadmap used by the corporation to keep on track with its corporate purpose. It outlines the roles of each part of the corporate structure, from the shareholders to the officers and employees, thereby setting who does what and when. In closely held corporations, it is also usual to see a "shareholders' agreement" being put into play. This document zeroes in on the rights and obligations of a shareholder and typically limits the rights a shareholder may have to sell or otherwise divest himself or herself of the stock. For a closely held business this means that a shareholder cannot sell the shares to an unknown third party without the corporation and other shareholders being first made aware of the transaction and without first giving permission and, in many cases, the right to purchase the shares instead of selling them to the unknown party.

The Board itself does not exercise day-to-day control over the business. Instead, it hires and then directs the officers of the corporation (the president, vice president, treasurer, and secretary) to take the Board's mandates and translate them into the actions needed to operate. In turn, the officers direct the employees on each person's duties in regard to his or her employment. Note again that technically, the shareholder has no active role in the day-to-day operations of the business. A shareholder interacts with the corporation only at the once-a-year annual meeting (or any special meetings), at which time the shareholders elect members to the Board and present issues that they want discussed.

The preceding description is how middle to large corporations operate. But remember, most franchisee business entities are closely held. In reality then, the shareholders are also the Board, the officers, and the employees. So, the question becomes whether a closely held business entity can ever operate as a corporation. The answer, of course, is yes. It is done all day, every day. Each person wears several hats, which are changed as the situation requires.

Subchapter S Corporation vs. Subchapter C Corporation

All corporations large or small have the same basic components and operate day-to-day in the same way. So why are we always hearing about "sub-S" corporations or "sub-C" corporations? Simply put, these designations are the names given by the IRS to two different corporation-taxing schemes and, for our purposes here, are relevant *only* for that purpose.

It is the job of the Board to determine how the corporation should be taxed, and there are myriad reasons to choose one over the other. For the closely held franchisee corporation, the Subchapter S corporation is the go-to entity. The advantage of the Subchapter S is that it allows the profits and losses of the corporation to flow directly to the shareholders without first being taxed at the corporate level. For a small business, this is a significant and indeed overwhelming reason to make this choice. There are, however, certain requirements that must be met if the corporation is to be taxed as a Subchapter S:

- The corporation must file the necessary papers with the state, called the Articles of Incorporation, in order to create the corporation. A corporation does not exist in the absence of such filing.
- The corporation must be a *domestic* corporation, meaning that must be formed in one of the states.
- There can be only one class of stock. This means that there cannot be "preferred stock" and "common stock." Instead there is only "common stock."
- The number of shareholders is limited to 100 (in most franchise corporations there are usually less than 10 and often less than 5).
- The shareholders must be natural persons, or certain trusts and estates.
- The shareholders must elect to be treated as a Subchapter S

corporation within a certain period of time by filing a two-page document called Form 2553. While this is an issue in the sense that it takes some time to complete (perhaps 5 to 15 minutes), in fact, it can be now filed by fax or snail mail without any filing fee or other cost.

A Subchapter C corporation does not have the limitations imposed on an S corporation. Here are the requirements if the corporation is to be taxed as a Subchapter C corporation:

- The corporation must file the necessary papers with the state (or foreign country of origin), most often called the Articles of Incorporation, in order to create the corporation. A corporation does not exist in the absence of such filing.
- The corporation may be a domestic corporation, or may be one originating in another country.
- There can be any number of classes of stock instead of being limited to one class. For instance, there can be shareholders that have the right to vote and shareholders who have no such right, and there can be shareholders who are preferred over other shareholders when it comes to distributing dividends.
- There is no limit to the number of shareholders—from 1 to 1,000,000 or more.
- The shareholders need not be natural persons or certain trusts and estates. Shareholders can be corporations, LLCs, trusts, sole proprietors, and foreign owners;
- An election with the IRS is not needed because the Subchapter C is the default taxation scheme.

Table 3.1. Corporation Comparison Chart

Attribute of Business Entity	S Corporation	C Corporation
Limited liability of owners	Yes	Yes
Permitted by all 50 states	Yes	Yes
Registration requirements	Yes	Yes
Duration	Perpetual or as defined	Perpetual or as defined
Required documents	Articles of Incorporation; and should have bylaws	Articles of Incorporation; and should have bylaws
Minimum number of owners	1	1
Identity of owners	Natural persons and some trusts and estates	Natural persons, trusts, estates, other limited liability business entities, corporations, partnerships, and others
Types of equity ownership	One class of shares only	Shareholders may be divided in any number of classes each having rights and duties different than the others.
Management	Board of Directors and officers. Shareholders, Board, and officers are often the same persons.	Board of Directors and officers. Shareholders, Board, and officers are often the same persons.
Election with the IRS	Yes	No. Default position with IRS is that of a Subchapter C corporation.
Consequence of no IRS election	Default to Subchapter C "double" taxation	No election needed
Pass-through taxation to the equity owners	Yes	No. Each dollar of the Subchapter C is taxed at the corporate level (paid by the corporation) and is then taxed on the individual level when it is paid to an employee as wages; or distributed to shareholders as dividends.
Corporate formalities	Yes. The corporation must adhere to the corporate formalities of the home state.	Yes. The corporation must adhere to the corporate formalities of the home state.
Required documents	Articles of Incorporation; and should have bylaws. Must elect with IRS to be treated as an S corporation within certain period of time.	Articles of Incorporation; and should have bylaws

It is not surprising then that most franchisees who elect to use the corporate structure choose the Subchapter S corporation.

Corporate Formalities

Regardless of the taxation method chosen, all corporations must follow the same formalities (often called the *corporate formalities*)

- Must file necessary documents to become a corporation
- Should have bylaws
- Must have at least an annual meeting of shareholders and Board
- Should hold "special meetings" at which significant business decisions are made
- Must keep minutes of all meetings
- Must have officers
- Should have certificates of shares (though some states have done away with this requirement)
- Must have list of shareholders
- Must maintain separate bank accounts
- Must honor fiduciary duties
- Must always sign documents and purchase goods and services in the corporate name

LIMITED LIABILITY COMPANY: BASIC STRUCTURE

The LLC was created to allow partners in a partnership or joint venture to enjoy the same veil of protection that shareholders of corporations enjoyed. Given its relatively young age (1977 to the present), confusion as to the purpose and operation of an LLC continues to perplex the general public.

First, the nomenclature is different. The "shareholders" of the LLC are called "members." In a corporation, there must be a Board of Directors and separate officers. Under an LLC, the members can serve both purposes (by electing to have the LLC "managed" by the members), or it can treat the members as being more passive investors by agreeing to have a "manager" (akin to the Board and officers) operate the LLC on a day-to-day basis.

Table 3.2. Corporate vs. LLC Personnel Comparison

Corporation	LLC
Shareholders	Members
Board of Directors	Members or manager
Officers	Members or manager
	LLC can have officers, directors, CEO, and so on

In addition, the bylaws of the corporation are replaced by a document called an "operating agreement," which serves the same purpose as the bylaws. The *operating agreement* provides directions on how to operate the business on a day-to-day basis and tells the members, managers, and others who will do what and when. In many cases, the operating agreement incorporates covenants restricting a member's right to transfer his or her interest. In this way it also functions as the shareholders' agreement.

LLCs can also choose the manner in which they are taxed. Originally, the LLC members were taxed only as *partners*, meaning that the same pass-through rights granted to partners were also granted to members, without being first taxed at the business-entity level. In this way, the LLC is akin to the Subchapter S corporation. Today, the LLC can elect to be taxed as a partnership or as a corporation. As with the S and C corporate taxation decision, there are reasons to choose between the options. In the franchise community, because of the closely held nature of most franchisee business entities, most franchisees choose to be taxed as a partnership.

As noted earlier, the LLC is not subject to the same statutory formalities requirements as a corporation. In most states, minutes of meetings are not required, certificates of ownership are not required, and even annual meetings are not required. At the IRS level, and unlike the corporation where the default position is taxation as a Subchapter C corporation (double taxation), the "default" position of an LLC is for taxation as a partnership. There is no need to "elect" such taxation as there is for the Subchapter S.

LLC Prerequisites

As with a corporation, in order to qualify as an LLC, the entity must follow guidelines:

- File the necessary papers with the state—most often called the Articles of Organization—in order to create the LLC. A limited liability business entity does not exist in the absence of such filing.
- The LLC can only be one that was created in the United States.
- There can be any number of classifications of members. As with Subchapter C, there can be voting and non-voting members, members that have a preference over other members, and the like.
- There is no limit to the number of members—from 1 to 1,000,000 or more.
- The members need not be natural persons, or certain trusts and estates. Shareholders can be corporations, LLCs, trust, sole proprietors, and foreign owners.
- The LLC does file tax documents as a way to acknowledge the taxation method it has chosen and to pay taxes at the business-entity level if it has chosen to be taxed as a corporation.

LLC Formalities

One of the benefits of an LLC over a corporation is that most states do not require the level of formality demanded of a corporation. In fact, most states do not require an annual meeting (though it is always suggested that you do so) and do not require minutes of meetings (though again, it is always suggested that you do so). Consider the following:

- Must file necessary documents to become a limited liability business entity
- Should have an operating agreement
- Should have at least an annual meeting
- Should have minutes of all meetings
- May have officers or may have members manage the business

- Certificates of ownership are not required (though it is a good idea to issue such certificates)
- Must have list of shareholders
- Must maintain separate bank accounts
- Must honor fiduciary duties
- Must always sign documents, purchase goods and services in the LLC name, and sign in your business-entity capacity (i.e. "member" or "manager")

Table 3.3 Subchapter S vs. LLC Comparison

Attribute of Business Entity	S Corporation	LLC
Limited liability of owners	Yes	Yes
Permitted by all 50 states	Yes	Yes
Registration requirements	Yes	Yes
Duration	Perpetual or as defined	Perpetual or as defined
Required documents	Articles of Incorporation; and should have bylaws. Must elect with IRS to be treated as an S corporation within certain period of time.	Articles of Organization; and should have operating agreement.
Minimum number of owners	1	1
Identity of owners	Natural persons and some trusts and estates	Natural persons, trusts, estates, other limited liability business entities, corporations, partnerships, and others
Types of equity ownership	One class of shares only	Members may be divided in any number of classes, each having rights and duties different than the others
Management	Board of Directors and officers. shareholders, Board, and officers are often the same persons.	Members or manager. May elect to have officers. Manager can be a member. *Members-managed* means has the right to bind the business in the same way as general partners.

Attribute of Business Entity	S Corporation	LLC
Election with the IRS	Yes	Yes, but only in the sense that you can "check the box" to elect to be taxed as a corporation
Consequence of no IRS election	Default to Subchapter C "double" taxation	Default to partnership taxation—pass through taxation
Pass-through taxation to the equity owners	Yes, once elected	Yes, if the LLC agrees to be treated as a partnership of tax purposes (meaning it doesn't opt to be taxed as a C corporation)
Corporate formalities	Yes. The corporation must adhere to the corporate formalities of the home state.	The LLC version of the corporate formalities is much less stringent. No annual meetings, no minutes, and the like.
Required documents	Articles of Incorporation and should have bylaws	Articles of Organization and should have operating agreement

There is another, more esoteric difference between the two entities, which in many cases goes to the heart of a closely held business arrangement: Under a corporation, if a shareholder is sued by a party for nothing having to do with the corporation (a car accident, for instance), and if the other party prevails, he or she as a "judgment creditor" has the right to take all of the shareholder's personal assets, including the shares of stock. If there is no shareholders' agreement or other arrangement that would require the other shareholders to purchase the shares from the judgment creditor, then the third party would step into the shoes of the shareholder and would by law become an owner of the corporation. Imagine the negative effect that would have on a closely held corporation! Indeed, if the shareholder were the majority shareholder, the judgment creditor interloper would be able to control the business.

In most states, under an LLC, this matter is somewhat eased. Under the same scenario as just mentioned, the third party would *not* take over the position of the member (with the right to vote, the right to manage, and an interest in the assets of the LLC) but instead would be allowed only to benefit from the member's profit and losses until such time as the third party's judgment is satisfied. Though, ultimately the judgment creditor may finally take over all membership rights of the member under certain circumstances, the presence of this limitation often protects the LLC from management by an unknown third party.

Most often, the franchisee will elect either a Subchapter S corporation or a limited liability company setup. Remember that a Subchapter S corporation can only elect to be taxed as a pass-through entity. On the other hand, with the check-the-box right that a LLC has to choose how to be taxed (as a Subchapter S, Subchapter C, or partnership), the franchisee may have greater latitude with the LLC. Once again, however, as often as not, franchisees choose to elect a Subchapter S status in no small part because most business people understand how a corporation works (with the Board of Directors, shareholders, officers, and bylaws), whereas the workings of an LLC (with members, managing members, managers, and the operating agreement) often seem mysterious.

In all cases, the business entity (be it a sole proprietorship, partnership, corporation, or LLC) must have both federal and state tax identification numbers before it may operate a business. The franchisee should check with his or her CPA for further information concerning this matter.

CORPORATION AND LLC FILING REQUIREMENTS

As previously noted, the creation of a corporate or LLC entity is determined at the state level. As a result, each of the 50 states has its own manner and method by which a corporation can incorporate or an LLC can organize. In the "prehistoric" days (before the internet), the franchisee had to file paperwork with, most often, the secretary of state in the state where the business was to open. This required the franchisee to hunt down the proper forms, figure out how to fill out the forms, write a check, and then mail everything to the secretary of state. It was not unusual for this process to take between two and six weeks. During that time, the franchisee could be sued in their personal capacity, thereby exposing personal assets to loss. Now virtually every state has a web portal that permits the franchisee to complete forms online, pay the filing fee with a credit card, and receive authorization to operate as a corporation or LLC either immediately or within 24 to 48 hours.

The choice of your business entity is a primary point of organization for the prospective franchisee. This should be part of your business plan and should be done only after consultation with the proper professionals.

Other Contracts

As a franchisee, you will be called upon to sign other contracts in addition to the franchise agreement. This section briefly reviews some of these contracts.

VENDOR CONTRACTS

An integral part of your operation of the franchised business is the purchase of all of your goods, supplies, and inventory through vendors approved by the franchisor. This is in brick-and-mortar setups as well as home-based operations. It will be most evident in a location-specific brick-and-mortar business such as a restaurant. When one goes into a McDonald's, everything the customer sees, from napkins and ketchup containers to menu boards and seating have all be purchased from the vendor system specifically approved by the franchisor. In many cases, it will be the franchisor or their affiliate that is nominated as the sole and only vendor, thereby giving the franchisor an additional revenue stream.

There is inherently nothing wrong with this arrangement. In fact, it is usual that the franchise system—acting as a single purchasing entity—will be able to purchase the goods and services below any other wholesale offering. Unfortunately, there have been in the past, and there certainly will be in the future, franchise systems that fail to put their "customers"—the franchisees—first and instead try to grab every last penny, even if it puts the entire franchise system at a competitive disadvantage. There can be nothing more upsetting than to purchase your vegetables from the approved vendor only to learn that you could have gone to a big retail operation and bought the same quality and quantity at a cheaper price.

Though you are required to use vendors approved by the franchisor, your contractual relationship is between the vendor and you and not between the franchisor and you. Thus, you must first read and then understand the contract of the contract.

> The best source for determining the value of the franchisor's vendor system is to talk with franchisees *before* you sign the franchise agreement.

Most vendor contracts are one to two pages long with a simple purchase order on the front and the so-called boilerplate, or fine print, on the back.

Since "the devil is in the details," it is usually not the front side of the vendor agreement that gets the franchisee in trouble—which just states that the supplier will deliver *x* loaves of bread every Tuesday for an agreed-upon sum. As you might imagine, it is the fine print on the back that causes the most headaches. For instance, the fine print could state that the supplier is permitted to deliver day-old bread; or, that in the event of any dispute, the parties would have to litigate in the hometown of the supplier that is 50 miles from the franchised business. Absent a claim of fraud or misrepresentation, every sentence of the small print is in most cases as enforceable as the language on the front side of the document. For that reason, the prudent franchisee keeps the number of his or her franchise attorney on speed dial.

Most vendor purchase orders will have the following covenants on the front side:

- Name and contact information of the vendor
- Name and contact information of the franchisee
- Space to list the goods, services, and supplies being offered

> Until the franchisee has had sufficient experience with contracts in general, the use of a franchise attorney is a good investment.

- Pricing grid showing the price per piece and the total price for each line item
- Statement of the purchase price for all of the goods, services, and supplies purchased

- Additional fees (if any) for taxes, delivery, and the like
- Final total purchase

As previously noted, it is the back side that contains the terms and conditions that the control the purchase. These covenants include the following:

- *Statement of Acceptance (or similar title).* The purpose of this covenant is the make it clear that the vendor will supply only the goods, services, and supplies specifically stated on the front side. It will not include any items that the franchisee may think should come with the order. For instance, ordering a supply of cabbage (which is usually identified by variety, quality size, and quantity) will not include any type of cabbage that falls outside the description, even though one could assume that smaller cabbages would be acceptable.

This same covenant may also state that the purchase order is not a contract between the parties unless and until the vendor accepts the agreement by signature on the document. The mere fact that the order was taken does not mean that it has been "accepted." It only means that the vendor has the option to accept, reject, or offer alternative goods, services, or supplies.

As with the franchise agreement, this statement may also specifically disclaim any oral agreements that were not reduced to writing on the front side of the document. If the salesperson promises to deliver fresh strawberries along with the cabbage, and you have created a menu item based on that promise, the fact that it was not stated in writing in the order means that the vendor may not be responsible for your failure to put it in writing. As with the "merger" covenant discussed in the franchise agreement review, the written purchase order "merges" any oral covenants, meaning that if it is not in writing, then it is not a contract obligation.

- *Statement of how the order may be amended.* In the absence of any language concerning an amendment, the vendor may simply refuse to allow any change to the order. In most cases, however, the agreement permits a change to be made: (i) up to a certain time before the order is to be delivered (for example, 24 hours); (ii) if it is in writing; and (iii) if it is accepted by the vendor. In some cases the vendor will add a charge not only for the added goods, services, or supplies, but also for the cost of making the change—usually expressed as a flat fee—for instance, $10 per accepted change.

- *Shipping and handling terms.* Most vendors' orders will disclose the manner and method of delivery. In the case of perishable goods, delivery will be by "refrigerated truck." If shipping and handling charges are stated on the front, then it will acknowledge that the cost is included as stated. If the type of good, service, or supply is such that these fees cannot be determined at the time of the order, the language should spell out how such fees will be calculated. If you are required to pay "COD"—either because you have no credit with the vendor or you have failed to make timely payments—then it will also state the terms of the COD delivery.

- *Right of inspection and rejection.* Anyone who has been in a retail business knows how important it is to immediately open and inspect each and every delivery. If the delivery is of perishable items, then such inspection should be done immediately upon delivery or as soon thereafter as is possible. If they are nonperishable goods, inspection should take place as soon as possible but usually no later than 24 hours. Though the law in most states (the "Uniform Commercial Code") spells out inspection periods that are longer than 24 hours, the fact is that the longer an inspection is held off, the more difficult it will be to make a claim. If an item is unacceptable for any commercially reasonable cause, then you have the right to reject the item. For instance, spoiled or nearly spoiled perishable goods should be rejected as should any items in a damaged retail box. On the other hand, if the box in which the goods or supplies is damaged but is not the box in which the goods will be displayed, and if the damage to the box did not cause damage to the goods, then there is no right to reject. Even if you have already paid, you have reasonable inspection/rejection rights.

- *Warranties.* Going hand-in-hand with the inspection/rejection rights will be the vendor's form of guaranty that the item delivered is fit for the purpose for which it was purchased (that is, a tomato is edible), and that it will be free from defects in materials and workmanship. If this warranty is violated, then the vendor will replace the damaged item with one in proper condition. If a reasonable inspection could not have discovered the defect, but the defect is later discovered, you may still be able to get the vendor to replace it.

- *Indemnification and insurance.* Once again, depending on the good, service, or supply being purchased, the vendor will insure the goods up to the point that they are delivered to you, and, subject to the warranty and right to inspect, you will be responsible for insurance once it hits your loading dock. In the case of an item that could cause personal injury to the end user (food, for instance), most vendors will also insure that the end user (your customer) will be covered if the product turns out to cause harm. Though the injured person would sue you as the franchisee, you could in turn bring in the vendor under this covenant and can seek to be protected from the loss. Of course, proving that it was solely the vendor's fault, and not your fault that the injury occurred is one that the courts must decide. Having the insurance, however, is better than not having it.

- *Additional provisions.* As with the franchise agreement, the vendor's contract will contain a statement that the contract is controlled by the laws of a certain state (which in the case of a national vendor system may not be your state), that time is of the essence, and that the franchisee is not to disclose the terms of the vendor agreement.

TRANSFER AND ASSIGNMENT AGREEMENTS

A *transfer* or *assignment* in the franchise world means that you are selling to another person or entity substantially all of your assets in the franchised business, your rights in the franchise agreement, or any combination of the two. Though there are any number of permutations of a transfer and an assignment, in either case, you must get your franchisor's prior permission to do so. This section assumes you have such permission and discusses the basic structure of such a transaction.

ASSET PURCHASE AGREEMENT

The transfer of your franchised business requires that you enter into special contracts. You can transfer only the assets of your business (including all pieces of furniture, fixtures, equipment, and other goods you use to operate the business) along with the business goodwill as a continuing commercial venture and the right for the buyer to continue the business (subject to the franchisor's approval), or you can transfer your entire interest in your franchise business entity, which means you are transferring all of your shares of stock (in the case of a corporation) or all of your interest in a limited liability business entity to a third party.

The first method is accomplished through the execution of an *asset purchase agreement*, in which you agree to sell all of the assets of your business to a third party, whereas the second method is done through an *equity transfer agreement*, in which you transfer your equity interest in the business (be it the shares of stock in a corporation or your membership interest in a limited liability company) to the third party. Under the asset purchase agreement, the purchaser is only purchasing the assets, goodwill, and right to operate the business—but none of the liabilities (except for the assumption of the franchise agreement). In the equity transfer transaction, the purchaser is stepping into your shoes, is purchasing all of your assets, and is assuming all of your liabilities. As a result, a vast majority of franchise transfers are done through the use of the asset purchase agreement—most buyers have no interest in taking over the seller's liabilities. We will briefly review the asset purchase agreement.

There is no set form for an asset purchase agreement, though as with the franchise agreement, all such agreements will have common elements, including the following:

- *Opening paragraph.* Names the parties to the transaction. The "Seller" is the franchisee, and the "Purchaser" (or "Buyer") is the third party.

- *The Recitals.* Often a contract will contain Recitals, which are usually a series of paragraphs that identify what each party's position is in the transaction and that acknowledge that the Seller is a franchisee of the franchise system. These paragraphs are not considered part of the binding covenants unless they are later "incorporated" into the contract by language to that effect.

- *The Assets.* The description of the assets should be a complete statement of what is being included in the sale. This will include not only hard assets (tables, chairs, and inventory) but also any "soft" (intangible) assets that are not otherwise owned by the franchisor. Remember that your business is identified with the franchisor's Marks and intellectual property. Although you can transfer your limited rights to the franchise agreement (indeed that will be one of the items described as an asset), you are not transferring any ownership rights in the Marks or intellectual property.

- *Statement of the liens or encumbrances that secure the assets.* In some cases, the franchisee/seller will have purchased the asset with a business loan. In that case, the lender will have placed a lien against assets in the form of a UCC-1 financial statement and a *security agreement.* The former is a document that is filed with the state and that notifies the world that the assets are encumbered. The latter is the document that lays out your obligations in reference to the assets—such as making sure that the assets are always insured and that each asset is properly maintained. If the assets are secured in this manner, then as part of the sale the seller will have to pay off the loan, or the buyer will have to assume the loan. In most cases, the seller will be required to pay off the loan so the assets can be transferred free and clear.

- *Statement of the business contracts that the buyer is assuming.* As you have learned in this chapter, a franchisee signs a myriad of contracts in order to operate the business. In each case, the buyer will be required to assume each such contract. A usual prerequisite to this process is the delivery of notice from the franchisor that the buyer is or will shortly become a franchisee. In such a case, the vendor will almost always grant the assignment. The assumption of other contracts that are not integral to the franchise—a contract to supply music for instance—will be negotiated between the parties.

- *A statement concerning any real estate leases.* The contract will also disclose how a real estate lease is to be handled. If the lease does not contain the assumption language that is otherwise required by the franchise agreement (see preceding item), then the buyer will have to negotiate with the landlord to take over the lease. This should be a "condition" to closing the deal, meaning that the lease matter must be resolved before the asset purchase deal is closed. If this condition cannot be satisfied, then the buyer will not be required to purchase the assets.

- *The "bill of sale" covenant.* Assets are transferred by a bill of sale. This covenant identifies that requirement and then affirms that the exact bill of sale to be used is attached as an exhibit. The bill of sale assures the buyer that the assets being purchased will be transferred free and clear of all lien or encumbrances *or* that the assets will be transferred subject to some *lien* (like the lien from the lender that gave the franchisee money to purchase the assets) or *encumbrance* (like the language in the franchise agreement that may prevent the buyer from selling the assets in the future). Attached as an exhibit to the bill of sale is the same list of assets that was identified in the first paragraph of the covenants.

- *Price.* The agreement will of course, state the price and the terms of payment—which is usually the requirement that the price be paid (subject to adjustments) on the date of closing.

- *Earnest money.* The covenant concerning the price usually includes the requirement that the buyer pay the seller a percentage of the purchase price as a good faith gesture of the buyer's serious ("earnest") intent to close the deal. This is paid at the time the agreement is signed and is either credited towards the entire purchase price if the deal closes, returned to the buyer if the buyer timely terminates the deal (see the upcoming "Conditions" item), or retained by the seller if the buyer fails to close after all conditions have been waived.

- *Owner carryback.* While the goal is always to have the entire purchase price paid at the time of closing, it is often the case that the buyer will not have all of the funds to do so, in which case the franchisee will agree to "carryback" the balance in the form of a promissory note. The promissory note is usually secured by the very assets that are being transferred. In that way, the seller can reclaim the assets should the buyer fail to make payments on the note. Though this arrangement can cause an issue with the assignment back to the franchisee of the franchise agreement—which scenario must be covered with the franchisor if there is a carryback—it is done in the franchise setting and is a fair way for the franchisee/seller to protect his or her sale.

- *Prepaid expenses.* It is usual for the franchisee/seller to have prepaid for certain expenses related to the operation of the business—utilities and rent are just a couple of these expenses. The prepaid expense often covers a period of time that straddles the closing of the purchase. In that case, the price will be adjusted to account for period of time the seller used the service before the closing and buyer used the service after the closing.

- *Inventory.* In virtually all cases, the franchisee/seller will have purchased inventory that will be used both before and after the closing. In that case, the parties usually agree to take an inventory count the day before the closing and then agree that the buyer will increase the price by the seller's cost (but not cost plus profit) for all useable inventory.

- *The allocation.* The seller and buyer in the asset-sale transaction must report the matter to the IRS and to the state. Under tax law, one asset may be taxed differently than another. For instance, the goodwill transferred is taxed differently than the computer that was also transferred. Further, the taxation benefits afforded the seller may conflict with the tax benefits that are available to the buyer. As a result, the allocation is negotiated and that is then reduced to writing. Make sure that you talk with your tax advisor to get the best advice on this matter.

- *Conditions or contingencies to buyer's obligation to close.* In addition to any other conditions previously called out in the asset purchase agreement, there will usually be a covenant that recites additional conditions that must be satisfied prior to buyer being obligated to close. These conditions usually include: (i) the right to inspect all of the assets; (ii) the right to review all contracts and other business records; (iii) the right to review the franchise documents and arrange for assumption of the franchise rights before the closing; (iv) the right to inspect and audit the financial books and records of the seller; (v) the right to determine whether the purchase of the assets and the assumption of the franchised business is a sound and "feasible" business decision; and (vi) similar inspection and evaluation rights. The buyer is usually given a stated period of time (such as ". . . for a period of 10 days after seller has delivered all of the

stated requirements . . ." or ". . . no later than 5 days before closing
. . .") in which to complete its investigation and then notify seller
that the conditions are satisfied and the buyer will proceed to closing, the buyer is dissatisfied and the buyer is terminating the contract—in which case the earnest money is returned, or the buyer is
willing to negotiate the price or other terms of the asset purchase
agreement in exchange for waiving an objectionable condition.

- *Seller's representations and warranties.* Both buyer and seller make
certain statements in the contract in order to assure the other
party of his or her ability to close the deal. The seller's representations and warranties include such affirmations that: (i) seller
indeed owns the assets and has the power to sell them; (ii) that
the purchase of the assets is subject to approval by the franchisor and assumption of the franchise agreement by the buyer; (iii)
that all taxes associated with the business have been paid; (iv) that
employees are not (or are) subject to employment agreements; and
(v) similar statements. These representations and warranties are
usually required to be true not only at the time the asset purchase
agreement is signed, but are also true at the time of closing. These
representations and warranties survive the closing and retain the
continuing declarations of the seller.

- *Buyer's representations and warranties.* Though usually a shorter list
than those of the seller, the buyer will represent and warrant that:
(a) the buyer has the power and authority to purchase the assets and
to close; and (b) the purchaser agrees that he or she must assume
the real estate lease, the contracts identified as being assumable, and
that the buyer must have made arrangements with the franchisor.

- *Continuation-of-business covenants.* The asset purchase agreement
will often include statements to the effect that the seller will continue to operate the business in its usual and normal course as
though the asset purchase agreement was not signed. In this way,
the buyer can be assured of getting the opportunity to take over

a business that is generating money in the same way that it was before the sale was even contemplated.

- *Indemnification covenants.* All asset purchase agreements will contain indemnification covenants. *Indemnification* means that the buyer and seller will reimburse the other for any losses suffered as a result of some negligent act or wrongdoing of the buyer or seller relating to the terms of the asset purchase agreement. In the case of the seller, he or she agrees to indemnify the buyer if: (i) any of the representations and warranties prove to be false; (ii) any of the assets proves to be in a condition other than as represented; (iii) the buyer incurs a loss after the closing that occurred as a result of some matter that occurred before the closing (for example, a customer slips and falls before the closing but does not sue until after the closing); or (iv) any other seller covenant of the asset purchase agreement proves to be inaccurate (for example, that there exists a previously undisclosed contract that negatively impacts one or more assets or the seller's ability to sell). Buyer's covenants include the promise of indemnification: (i) if the buyer's representations and warranties turn out to be false; and (ii) if the seller is brought into a lawsuit for something that happens after the closing (for example, the buyer's failure under the lease).

- *Covenant concerning the closing.* This will call out the date, time, and place of the closing and will reiterate each party's obligations at the time of closing (for example, the seller agrees to sign the bill of sale, and the buyer agrees to pay the price).

- *Default provision.* The buyer and seller will agree upon the rights that each has in the event that the other party breaches the contract before closing. It is usual for the seller to retain the earnest money as its sole and only remedy (called a *liquidated damages* covenant), while the buyer will have the right to seek monetary damages, or the right to force the seller to sell (called the *specific performance* remedy), or the right to both remedies.

- *Additional provisions.* The same "additional provisions" found in the franchise agreement, the vendor's contract, and in virtually all other contracts will in some form be included here.

FRANCHISE ASSIGNMENT AGREEMENT

The franchisor will have a say in whether the proposed asset purchase will in fact be permitted to close. Virtually all franchise agreements require the franchisee to get the franchisor's prior written permission before proceeding with an asset purchase (or equity purchase) agreement. As noted previously, the franchisor will want to vet the proposed buyer/new franchisee in the same manner that measures the qualifications of all other prospective franchisees. Assuming the person is approved, the franchisor will prepare a franchise assignment agreement or franchise assumption agreement. Such agreements usually contain the following terms:

- The proposed buyer/new franchisee will be required to take and pass franchisor's initial training.
- The seller/franchisee or buyer/new franchisee will have to pay the transfer fee.
- The proposed buyer/new franchisee may be required to sign the then-current franchise agreement.
- The proposed buyer/new franchisee will be required to renovate the brick-and-mortar to the then-current specifications.
- The seller/franchisee will have to sign a general release.

In the brick-and-mortar franchise, the franchisee will be required to sign a lease. This is covered more extensively in the next chapter.

As you can imagine, the intricacies of contracts is something that one learns in law school and then spends a career trying to understand. Though you should carefully read each contract that you sign, you should never undertake this process without the help of a franchise lawyer and accountant.

Employees

What has been true in the past remains true today: Good employees are a treasure that can boost the profile and profit of a business. The inverse is, unfortunately, also true: a bad employee can ruin your reputation and can sink your business. Hiring, training, retaining, and firing employees is a book unto itself, but there are some legal generalities that we cover in this section. We discuss more employment tips in Chapter 7.

WHAT YOU CAN'T ASK

Federal law and state statutes in all 50 states prohibit an employer from discriminating against a potential hiree. We all have heard the list: "You cannot discriminate based on race, color, creed, national origin, or religion." That list, however, is outdated and incomplete. Not only are you prohibited from discriminating against those classes, you are also prohibited from discriminating because of a person's name; ancestry; sexual orientation; age; marital, parental, or family status; or a person's disabilities (though it is fair to ask whether the person is capable of performing the essential functions of the job). Some states have even more categories.

It seems that there should be a defined list of the exact questions that one should ask and that one is prohibited from asking. Unfortunately, there is not. But here are some of the basic matters.

Do not ask:

- *About religion.* It is never relevant. Instead, ask the person what days he or she is available to work.

- *What religious holidays they can work.* Again, it is not relevant. Ask instead whether the person is available to work on the days that the business needs the person.

- *About ethnic origin.* A person's background, though interesting, is not the subject of a job interview. If it is at all important to the job, ask the person what languages he or she is proficient in. If it is not important to the job, then don't even ask that.

- *About citizenship.* Though this seems counterintuitive, the fact is that the person's citizenship is not important. Ask instead whether the person is authorized to work in the United States. If the person is hired, he or she will have to prove this ability by filing out employee verification documents.

- *About clubs or social affiliations.* Though volunteering is important, and one's social affiliations are interesting, asking the question can reveal a person's political, ethnic, or religious beliefs. Ask instead whether the person is a member of any professional groups that are relevant to the job.

- *A woman her maiden name.* This obviously elicits an answer about her marital status. You can ask whether she has had job experience under another name.

- *About children.* It is not relevant. If the job includes children as a component, it is fair to ask if the person has had any experience with children in the relevant age groups.

- *About plans to have children.*

- *About marital status.*

- These are just some questions that call for careful consideration. Your local chamber of commerce, state department of employment, and Small Business Administration all have more information available on the internet.

HIRING A NEW EMPLOYEE: LEGAL CONSIDERATIONS

Gone are the days when you simply sat the new employee down at a desk and told them what to do. This section talks about procedures that must be followed. Some are federal, state, or local requirements, and others are common sense demands:

- *Obtain a federal Employer Identification Number (EIN).* This is a number given to you by the IRS. It is used to track your tax obligations for each employee. The EIN can be obtained online by going to the IRS website.

- *Set up accounting books for each employee.* There are several great accounting software programs that have already done the legwork by setting up the categories needed for each employee. Your franchisor may already have given you the name of the program that it requires you to use. If not, talk with other franchisees about the software systems they use.

You are responsible for accounting for and then paying federal income tax withholding for each employee, preparing and filing federal wage and tax statements, preparing and filing state and local wage and tax statements, and generally accounting for sick leave, vacation, and other financial matters that affect the employee's wages and pay.

- *Verify each employee's eligibility to work in the United States.* Each employee must complete the form I-9, which is readily available online. In most cases, it can be filled out online as well. Once the I-9 has been completed, the employer must verify the information contained in the document. This can be done manually by reviewing an employee's citizenship or visa documents (for example, a birth certification, passport, visa, or the like), or the employee can sign up for the U.S. Immigration and Customs Enforcement Agency's E-Verify program.

- *Report each new or rehired employee to the federally mandated and state-maintained "State Directory of New Hires."* Each state must have this directory.

- *Obtain workers compensation insurance.* You may think that because your business requires the employee to only sit at a desk, or because you have only one employee, that you do not need workers compensation. Neither supposition is true. Once again, each state has specific laws and regulations governing workers compensation insurance. Your failure to have it may violate the law and may result in your personal liability for a workplace injury.

- *Post the required notices.* You may have seen posters in break rooms or other locations where employees meet. These are giant reminders to the employees of their rights and are federally mandated and state-specific. There are a number of online resources for these posters.

- *File your tax forms.* Though it seems self-evident, many new employers fail to file their employee-based tax forms in a timely manner. Talk with your accountant about this and ask for help in setting up a reminder system to insure proper filing.

AT-WILL EMPLOYEES VS. EMPLOYEES WITH CONTRACTS

An employee can be hired without a contract or with a contract. Most employees in a franchise setting are hired without a contract—and for good reason. In the absence of a written contract, an employee can quit a job for any reason or no reason, and an employer can fire (or "separate from employment") an employee for any reason or no reason. Once a contract is signed, however, the employee gains not only the rights contained in the contract, but also other implied rights that may in the end make transferring the employee or even firing them very difficult. That is not to say that written contracts should not be used for specific jobs or personnel. Instead, such contracts should be very limited in use and in scope and should be created only after talking with an employment law specialist.

RECORD-KEEPING

Record-keeping is a pain! There are no two ways about it. During a busy day, at the end of a grueling shift, or late at night, the last thing someone wants to do is write down what happened during the day. Yet there can be no better insurance in an employee dispute than to have good records. After any substantive meeting with an employee, write down what was talked about and what the resolution was. Such meetings include not only one-on-one meetings about the employee's performance, but should also include strategy meetings. Show it to the employee to insure that you both heard the same thing. If there are minor complaints, complete a reasonable investigation and write down the results. If there are major complaints about the employee's demeanor, work product or the like, it may be time to talk with your employment law expert about the next steps.

EMPLOYEE MANUALS

An employee manual is the classic rock-and-hard-place conundrum. Not many employers understand that the manual is in fact a contract. As we discussed previously, you want to avoid contracts. Yet how can you express company policies and practices unless they are in writing? The truth is that a well-written employee manual is a critical employment management tool. Without it, the employer runs the risk of being sued because of perceived unequal or discriminatory treatment between employees. Yet with it, the employer must then follow what was written. Even for a one-employee operation, an employee manual is critical. It need not be a long document in that case, but the basics should nonetheless be spelled out. This is again the place that your employment law expert will be needed. Your manual should conform with federal and state law and should cover all areas of general importance to the operation of your business. Manuals usually include topics on the following:

- Nondiscrimination in practice and in fact. Make it clear that the workplace will not tolerate discrimination in any form. This is not only the law, it is the right thing to do.
- Policy on sexual harassment. The prohibition of sexual harassment is not only the law, once again, it is the right thing to do.
- Dress code. If dress is critical to the business, then it should be spelled out.
- Work hours and break times.
- Use of computers and telephones (including the employee's cell phone) for non-business use.
- Theft and dishonesty.
- Use of legal and illegal drugs and alcohol on the job.
- Smoking policy.

- Violence in the workplace.
- Probationary period rules.
- Performance evaluations.
- Payment matters.
- General safety matters.
- Complaint procedures, including warnings and termination rules.
- Benefits given to workers.

Good employer-employee relationships are central to a successful business. Work with your franchisor and employment law expert to create a workplace that is safe, fun, and profitable.

Conclusion

As amazing as it may sound, very few franchisees read the contracts that create the franchise relationship or that are used in the operation of the business. For a layperson, a long legal document is intimidating. Be sure to have a clear understanding of any and all of your legal relationships.

Money spent on professional help may be expensive at the time, but in truth, it is money well spent. At the end of the day, you will have an intimate understanding of the who, what, when, where, and why of the franchise relationship and will be better able to protect your interests.

Franchise Finance and Funding

Having a strong grasp on your businesses financial health is mission-critical for success. This chapter begins with an overview of startup funding and financing tips and strategies so you can start your business the right way. Later in this section you will learn about business finance principals so you can run your business with sound financial elements in place.

Obtaining Startup Financing or Funding

Underfunding is one of the most common reasons that new businesses fail. It is mission-critical to make sure that you obtain adequate funding to launch and grow your business.

Your business plan is a starting point for projecting a realistic budget (expenses) for your business as well as your best estimate of probable revenue (income). You may have heard people say that it always costs more than you think, which is true in many cases due to underestimating costs.

BUSINESS PLAN

Your business plan serves many purposes as you prepare to launch your new business. Some think that you only need a business plan if you are trying to raise capital via investors or bankers. Even though this is one reason, you will find that a comprehensive business plan will help you in many ways such as:

- *Focus.* You will find that you have to tie up all the loose ends and think through all elements of your business in detail, which clarifies your overall business vision.
- *Advisors.* Many successful entrepreneurs believe in "paying it forward" by giving advice to new business owners. Your business plan gives them a snapshot of your business to work from.
- *Partners.* You can attract and educate possible business partners.
- *Raising money.* Still the most common application since most financial investors and bankers need to see that you have a solid business that will be able to pay them back.

Here are some tips on creating a business plan:

- Create a short "executive summary" version (three to five pages) as an introduction to pique the reader's interest so they can decide to invest more time to read the longer version.
- Use an online business plan builder tool to expedite the process.
- Keep your projections conservative.

- Make sure you are telling a cohesive story and not just filling in the blanks. It must be compelling to the reader.
- Obtain a basic non-disclosure agreement (NDA) to have recipients sign if you are going to include sensitive proprietary information for added protection of your trade secrets.
- When raising capital, be careful that you do not break any securities laws by seeking the advice of a qualified securities attorney.
- Don't make the mistake of assuming that you do not need a business plan since you are buying a franchise and not starting a business from scratch.
- Don't expect your franchisor, or prospective franchisor, to help you with the creation of a business plan. This is an exercise for you to achieve.

> You can find assistance for writing your business plan at www.franchisebiblestudy.com.

SELF-FUNDING

You may find that funding your business with your own money is the best option. This may mean you have to start smaller and scale up over time. Many banks are more willing to lend to a business that has a track record and cash flow, so getting "open for business" may be a good strategy for future funding for growth.

Banks consider a business a speculative venture and riskier when it is "pre-revenue" or still in the idea stage. Consider the following:

- You can begin by building business credit with very small accounts.
- Outsource services instead of hiring "in-house" staff to keep costs down initially.
- Keep track of your initial investments into your company for accounting purposes.

PARTNERS

Some say that business partnerships are like a marriage without the romance. Many partnerships end badly, unfortunately. It is typical for partners to start out on the same page due to a common interest and pure enthusiasm. A successful partnership must be able to weather difficult and stressful times.

- Be sure to choose partners based on what they can bring to the table to build the business beyond simply putting some money in the bank.
- Begin with very clear and defined roles and responsibilities for all partners.
- Be sure to hire a qualified business attorney to draft a partnership agreement including a buy-sell agreement.

General Financing Options

It is very common for new business owners to utilize one or more financing options to fund their business startup and growth. You can apply the tips in this section to help you navigate the many programs that are available today.

CONVENTIONAL LOANS

Standard banks and other lending institutions will offer a variety of conventional loan options. These loans include Small Business Administration (SBA) loans, business and personal loans, and credit lines as well as credit card programs:

- Begin building a relationship with your banker the very first day that you open your business bank account.
- Dress to impress when you meet with loan officers.
- Fill out applications completely and provide all of the support materials requested.
- Make sure conventional loans are the best option before you apply with multiple inquiries on your credit bureau, which can hurt your effort.

EQUIPMENT LEASES

Many businesses use equipment, such as kitchen equipment for a restaurant, or a work truck for an electrician, that can make up a large portion of the build-out or startup costs of a new franchised business. You will find a variety of leasing options for business equipment:

- Be sure to seek the advice of a qualified accountant or CPA to discuss the pros and cons of leasing as well as tax ramifications and possible benefits of leasing.
- Leases come in a variety of structures, and not all are advantageous, so do your research to understand all of the details.
- Try to hold the account in your business name to build credit for your business entity.

SELF-DIRECTED 401K AND IRA OPTIONS

Some business owners utilize the self-directed 401K or IRA to fund a business venture:

- Discuss the pros and cons with an accountant that has experience with these programs.
- Make sure that you have all of the information on how to properly set this up so you don't pay penalties.
- Get professional help to make sure you stay in compliance with the program rules.

Creative Finance Options

Startup businesses are sometimes categorized as speculative ventures by financial institutions even if they are associated with a franchise concept. This is usually due to the fact that the performance of the new owner and the franchise concept in a new location or market is new location or market is as-yet unproven.

ANGEL INVESTORS

Angel investors are people that may lend or gift you money because they believe and care about you, and not primarily for a business investment. Usually friends and family members are more likely to take a chance based on who you are and care less about the actual business investment or return on investment (ROI):

- Be careful to only take money from people that understand that it is a business transaction, even if they are friends and/or family.
- Be sure they can afford to invest and lose the money if it doesn't work out.
- Use contracts such as promissory notes or other agreements to spell out the details of the arrangement.

EB5 INTERNATIONAL INVESTOR PROGRAM

EB5 is a U.S. government program that allows international investors to invest in American companies. The program requires that the American company creates new jobs, and the investor can earn a U.S. green card.

- Seek the advice of an experienced EB5 attorney.
- Make sure you can meet the capital requirements to initiate the EB5 process and that the scope of your project is appropriate for the program.
- Be sure that your business will be able to generate the required number of jobs in the allotted time frame.

CROWDFUNDING

Crowdfunding or "crowd sourcing" is a newer phenomenon that has raised millions of dollars for businesses as well as for other projects. This platform allows an individual or company to set up an online profile with an overview of the project including the target amount of capital to be raised. Different states have a variety of rules, laws, and regulations that need to be carefully considered before attempting a crowdfunding effort:

- Research the state and federal laws to determine the feasibility of crowdfunding for your business.
- Make sure you can put together a comprehensive plan to market

the opportunity in such a way that you reach a big enough audience to raise the target amount.

- Be sure to tell your story in a compelling way.

Commit to Financial Literacy

Once you obtain your startup funding you will want to create a comprehensive budget for your business. This is also a good time to increase your knowledge of business finance.

BUDGETING

You can find many business budgeting tools that can help you design and track your business budget. Choose the tools that best suit your business and management style. Surprisingly, many business owners have little or no idea what is going on with the financial health of their businesses. Here are some tips:

- Begin your budget plan immediately. Don't wait until some point in the future that may never come. Every day that you operate without a budget in place can cost you dearly.
- Compare the "real numbers" against your budget on a regular basis to track progress.
- Be flexible. It is okay to adjust as you go as long as the numbers continue to make sense.
- Share your budget with your financial experts and let them help.
- Be disciplined and stick to your budget plan even when it is hard.

FINANCIAL KNOWLEDGE IS POWER

Every penny counts in business. Making consistent wise decisions can enable you to increase your profits and reduce your costs, which usually results in a healthy, thriving business. You will find many options for finance education online and from a variety of institutions. You don't necessarily need an accounting degree, but a solid operational understanding in this area is a plus.

You can also interview and hire experts such as accountants, CPAs, and financial planners to help you build a strategy for your business and family. Remember to factor in items that you may have the tendency to take for granted when working as an employee, such as your own benefits and retirement plan.

It has been said that it is not how much you make, but how much you spend, that determines the success of a business. Many businesses make a lot of money and never show a profit. Keeping a close eye on your company financials will give you an advantage when it comes to managing your money.

BOOKKEEPING, ACCOUNTING, AND FINANCIAL STATEMENTS

Good recordkeeping is essential for every business. There are many affordable online bookkeeping and accounting software platforms that you may consider, unless your franchisor offers a custom solution, which will be more suited for your business.

These platforms will allow you to manage daily income and expenses for cash flow purposes and give your accountant or CPA access for tax preparation and payroll. You will also be able to pull useful financial statements such as profit and loss (called the *income statement*) and balance sheet reports.

COST OF GOODS SOLD (COGS)

One of the common determinations that you will want to identify is the cost of goods sold or COGS within your business model. *This* is the accumulated total of all costs used to create a product or service that has been sold. This usually includes the materials and labor expenses to produce a product. Service businesses such as restaurants factor only the ingredients to deliver a finished food product to be sold but not the labor. These are considered *direct costs*. The COGS is subtracted from revenues to arrive at the gross margin of a business on the income statement, also known as the *profit and loss statement*.

OPERATING EXPENSES

Operating expenses are those expenditures that a business incurs to engage in any activities not directly associated with the production of goods or services. The simple way to think of this is the expenses to run your business above the COGS.

Good business managers are proficient at reducing these costs whenever possible to increase profitability. An example is a restaurant manager sending servers home early during slow shifts to cut the labor expenses.

LABOR, SALARIES, BONUSES, AND BENEFIT COSTS

Labor cost must be factored into most business operations. You will want to figure out the actual labor cost, which includes the hourly wages, salaries, bonuses, and related taxes.

RENT OR MORTGAGE

Business models that have a storefront location or building are often referred to as brick-and-mortar businesses. These business models will incur additional expenses related to the physical location. The biggest of these expenses is the amount allocated to rent or mortgage payments.

ROYALTIES AND OTHER FEES

Franchise businesses have specific expenses that are to be paid to the franchisor and approved or required suppliers and/or vendors. These fees are itemized in item six of the franchise disclosure document. You will need to include these fees in your expense accounting and operating budget.

FRANCHISOR REPORTS

There are a variety of formats and programs that franchisors use for reporting. Some organizations are networked with the corporate office on a common *point of sales* (POS) system, while others may require reports that need to be filled out and sent in with the respective payments. Ask our franchisor what methods they use for reporting while you are investigating your franchise options.

EBITDA and Business Valuation

There are many methods of factoring a valuation of a business. A common starting point is to determine the company's *earnings before interest, taxes, depreciation, and amortization* (EBITDA), which is an accounting measure calculated using a company's net earnings, before interest expenses, taxes, depreciation, and amortization are subtracted. This figure is a snapshot of a company's current operating profitability. Depending on the type of business, a multiple of EBITDA can be used as a valuation of the business.

Conclusion

This chapter covered a variety of financing and funding options to consider. Apply these concepts as you create your startup funding strategy. Once you have obtained the necessary funds, you can move on to the next steps to launch your business. The financial management of your new business has many variables. You will want to work with your franchisor as well as a qualified accounting service to start your business on the right foot and grow with a strong financial plan in place.

CHAPTER 5

Location, Location, Location

Choosing the best real estate for your new business is one of the most important controllable factors that will impact your overall success potential. This is especially true if you are going to open a business that is dependent on being in a good location. For instance, some business models such as mobile services or appointment-based office types may not be affected as much by the location of the business, whereas a restaurant or retail business may succeed or fail based on the location. This section gives you an overview of the real estate side of starting your franchise. It is a good idea to learn as much as you can about this subject.

We have found that many new franchise owners do not possess experience in commercial real estate and end up making costly mistakes. The franchisor may give you guidelines and assistance, but the best strategy to make sure that you get the best possible deal is to be educated and align with experts that will help you negotiate.

Real Estate Leases

Once the franchisee has completed the site selection process, he or she will be ready to work with the landlord to secure an acceptable commercial lease. Like so many other contracts, there are no "form" or "standard" leases, and a landlord can fashion any contract they want. At the end of the day, though, market forces will result in the lease of one landlord being similar in the material content of neighboring landlords.

The length of the lease will depend on the type of commercial property being leased. If you are leasing a space in a small strip mall, the leases tend to be a few dozen pages. If for an upscale mall, you can expect the lease to span 50 pages or more.

> Once again, the franchisee should not go it alone: This is the time to use the services of an experienced real estate lawyer who will help you understand the fine points of the lease.

Though you will use the services of an attorney, at the end of the day, it is the franchisee who will be responsible for understanding the lease and who will be called upon to perform under its terms; you have to read it! To help with that process, and remembering that like other contracts, there will be covenants that are common to all commercial leases, here are the major points to consider in reviewing a commercial lease. Also, take a look at online at www.entrepreneur.com/franchiseresources for a list of commonly used lease terms.

BASE PROVISIONS

The first section of most leases, called the Base Provisions, contains the general overview of the terms and conditions of the lease. For instance, it will identify by name and by contact information both the landlord and tenant. This section also includes the following:

- The identification of the Premises (sometimes called the Demised Premises) to be leased including the location in the center, the square footage, and any other identifying information.

- The Term (meaning the length of time) of the lease. This may be expressed as a number of months (for example, 60 months), a number of years (for example, five years) or a mixture of both.

- A statement of the base rent, the CAM (Common Area Maintenance) costs, and a statement of the tenant's pro rata share of CAM costs, landlord's insurance, real estate taxes, and the like. Tenant's pro rata share is usually determined by a fraction, the numerator of which is the tenant's square footage (usually identified as the "rentable square footage"), and the denominator of which is the square footage of all rentable areas of the property. All of the quoted terms in this paragraph are defined in online at www.entrepreneur.com/franchiseresources.

- A statement of the tenant's security deposit. The security deposit is used to insure the full and faithful performance of the tenant under the lease.

- A statement of the permitted use. The permitted use is literally the use for which the tenant is renting the property—be it a pizza restaurant or a children's clothing store.

- The identification of the common areas (being those areas that are used in common for the benefit of all tenants, including walkways, parking lots, stairwells, and the like) for which the CAM cost is calculated.

Following the Base Provisions will be the covenants that spell out the tenant's specific rights and duties, using specific terms and language. They will include the following:

- *The Grant.* This section will state that the tenant is being granted the right to use the Premises.
- *The Term.* This section will expand upon the Base Provisions by identifying the date of delivery of the Premises to the tenant (which may or may not signal the start of the Term), by calling out reasons for a delay in the delivery of the Premises to the tenant, and similar matter.
- *Condition of the Premises.* This section will go over the condition of the Premises at the time that it is delivered to the tenant. It may state that the Premises is fully built-out and ready to open its doors, or more often, it will identify it as a "vanilla shell" or some similar term and will then discuss what the tenant must do in terms of work in order to bring the Premises to a fully rentable condition.
- *Landlord and tenant work.* In most cases, the lease will provide that the landlord will deliver the Premises to the tenant with basic work already completed. This usually includes a statement that the walls will be up (though they may not be dry-walled), that basic electrical, plumbing, and heating, ventilation, and air conditioning (HVAC) systems have been installed. The lease will then call out the work that the tenant has to complete in order to open its doors. This will include the final installation of all electrical, plumbing, HVAC, phone, computer system, and similar systems, the installation of lighting, flooring, walls and wall coverings, the installation of interior and exterior signs, and so on.

This section may also include the tenant's *finish allowance* (sometimes called the TI). To induce a tenant to sign a lease, many landlords will offer the *tenant incentive* money in the form of a reimbursement for part of the tenant's cost to build out the space. This is discussed earlier in this chapter.

- *Opening Date.* Most leases will require that the tenant be open no later than the stated date. This is sometimes called the Rent

Commencement Date, Opening Date, or just the Commencement Date.

- *Rent, Additional Rent, Percentage Rent. Rent* comes in many flavors. Most commercial leases will have several components that make up the total Rent, including the Base Rent and all items that are identified as Additional Rent. Such fees include the tenant's payment of their pro rata share of the CAM costs, the tenant's pro rata share of the real estate taxes assessed against the entire project, and the tenant's pro rata share landlord's insurance premiums paid in exchange for insurance on the entire project.

In some cases, the landlord will ask not only for the Rent, but will also ask for Percentage Rent, which means that the tenant will also pay a percentage of its revenue to the landlord. The landlord and tenant will first define the base number upon which to calculate the Percentage Rent. This usually is expressed as some milestone in the tenant's gross revenue. For instance, Percentage Rent may kick in only after the tenant has earned $1,000,000 in gross revenue during a calendar year. The next component will be the percentage of the Base that is to be paid. Again this is negotiated between the landlord and tenant and may range from 1 percent to 5 percent or more. Nationally recognized franchised businesses that are known for generating significant gross revenue may be made subject to a Percentage Rent covenant. Most small franchised businesses can negotiate this out of the contract.

- *Past Due Rent.* The lease will also spell out the consequences of missing a Rent payment. This can range from a mere penalty of a percentage of the missed payment (that is, 5 percent of the amount that was due) or a fixed dollar figure, to a combination of both along with other consequences. Such consequences can include the right of the landlord to take the Rent money directly out of the tenant's operating account through an electronic funds transfer, and can also include the requirement that the tenant pay the landlord's representative in person.

- *Security Deposit.* All leases will have an article that addresses the use of the Security Deposit. In most cases the covenant will require the tenant to maintain the amount of the deposit in case the landlord uses any portion of it to cure a tenant breach. At the end of the lease, the Security Deposit will be used by the landlord if the Premises are left in a condition that requires repairs above and beyond what would be expected. In that case, the landlord will return the portion of the Security Deposit that is not used. Most states require the landlord to return the Security Deposit (or a letter stating the reason that part of it was used), within 30–60 days.
- *Tenant's Obligations.* As a general catch-all covenant, the landlord may include a list of the tenant's general obligations concerning smoking, trash removal, compliance with laws, and the like.
- *Maintenance and Repairs.* The landlord will spell out in detail the tenant's Maintenance and Repair obligations. Typically, the tenant is responsible to maintain and repair when necessary each and every system located within the Premises including the plumbing, electrical, HVAC, walls, ceilings and floors, lighting, and the like. It is often said that the tenant is responsible for everything inwards from the first coat of paint on the walls. Even in the case where the landlord installed the item, the tenant will be responsible.

On the other hand, the landlord is typically responsible for the structural components of the Premises, like the roof and floor joists, any cement flat work, and the like. Such expenses will, however, be included in the CAM costs and will be spread out among the tenants through the pro rata payment of the CAM cost.

- *Common Area.* There will be substantial coverage concerning the Common Area. It will identify the components of the Common Area (including walkways, roof covering, the parking lot, public area lighting, and the like) and will state that all costs incurred for the maintenance, repair, and replacement of such items will be included in the CAM cost. This covenant will also reiterate the manner and method of calculating each tenant's pro rata share and will also identify the method by which it will be collected as Additional Insured.

- *Utilities.* This section will identify the utilities that are payable directly by the tenant and those that will be payable by the landlord, which will then be allocated to the landlord—which the landlord will pay as part of the CAM or that will be divided between tenants that actually use the utility.
- *Taxes.* The landlord passes the real estate tax burden for the entire project on to all of the tenants through a pro rata charge, which is identified as Additional Rent. This is usual.
- *Insurance.* The landlord will also pass on to the tenants, pro rata, the cost of all insurance premiums spent to insure the entire project.

Tenant's insurance obligations do not end there, however. The tenant will be required to purchase specific insurance policies to insure its operation of the franchised business and to insure against any hazard or other loss. This insurance will name the landlord (and usually the franchisor) as an Additional Insured. The named Additional Insured piggybacks on the tenant's insurance and is covered from loss in the same manner and to the same extent as the Named Insured—that being the tenant/franchisee. The Additional Insured does not pay for this privilege, however. That is left to the tenant. Once again, this is usual.

- *Furniture, Fixtures, and Equipment (FF&E).* The lease will call out the requirements for the tenant's FF&E. For instance, the lease may require only new furniture and equipment. This may also be controlled by the franchise agreement. This same section will also account for the use of exterior and interior signs, and will identify what items are *trade fixtures* (those owned by the tenant) and what are *real estate fixtures* (those items that when attached by the tenant to the Premises become the landlord's property).

This covenant will also cover the fate of the FF&E upon expiration or earlier termination of the lease. In the former case, the tenant will be allowed to remove the trade fixtures but not the real estate fixtures. In the latter case, the landlord may exercise the right to a *landlord lien*, which gives the landlord the statutory right to keep the tenant's trade fixtures as security for the violation of the lease.

- *Hazardous Materials.* The lease will be specific in limiting the tenant's right to use, store, or generate hazardous materials or substances.
- *Damage by Fire, Hazard, or Other Loss.* This section will go over the rights and obligations of the parties in the case of loss by fire hazard or other occurrence. In many cases, if the Premises is only partially damaged, the lease may allow for the Premises to be reduced in size (if the tenant can still operate in a smaller footprint), and for the Rent to be equitably reduced as well.
- *Eminent Domain.* Eminent Domain is the right granted to the state or federal government (and to certain private individuals) to take another person's property for just compensation. Often called a *condemnation*, an Eminent Domain action requires the landlord and tenant to determine how their leasehold interests will be affected. In some cases the landlord may lose land, but the tenant's Permitted Use will be unaffected. In other cases, the lost property may affect the tenant's ability use the Premises for the purpose for which it was leased. In both cases, the landlord has a right to compensation to cover his or her loss. The tenant on the other hand has the limited right to seek damages. For instance, although the tenant can recover moving expenses and the loss of tenant finish, they cannot sue for loss of business opportunity or loss of profit.

- *Exclusive Use.* It is always worth negotiating for a covenant that gives the franchisee/tenant the right to be the sole and only business in the project that offers the franchisee's goods or services. For example, if the franchisee/tenant is a pizza restaurant serving salads, calzones, and beer and wine, then asking for an exclusive that will deny the landlord the right to lease to a similar use will be valuable. This will not prevent that the landlord from leasing to a burger joint, or even perhaps to the restaurant that makes only a small part of its revenue from the sale of pizza slices (for example, 10 percent or less of its gross revenue is from the sale of pizza), but it will give you the comfort of knowing that no direct competitor will be allowed into the space.

- *Assignment and Subletting.* As is the case with the franchise agreement, the landlord has made a business decision to lease the Premises to the tenant and not to another person. As a result, the landlord will closely control the tenant's right to assign the lease to a new tenant and will also have the right to limit the tenant's right to sublease the space. In both cases, the landlord will want the "old" tenant to remain liable under the lease—either in a secondary position in reference to the assignment, or in a primary position in reference to the sublease.

- *Default of Tenant Under the Lease.* This section will cover the landlord's position on breaches of the lease. Some breaches may be relatively minor, in which case the landlord will offer the tenant a limited right to cure the problem, but others will be major breaches for which no cure is granted. Thus, while the failure to pay on time may be a breach for which the tenant is given x number of days to cure from the date that the landlord sends notice, the tenant's destruction of the Premises, the assignment or subletting of the Premises without permission, or the closing of the business are all breaches for which immediate termination is the result.

- *Damages.* The Damages covenants may be part of the Default covenant or may be a standalone article. Upon breach of the lease the landlord will have the right to: (i) terminate the lease and seek damages for past events; (ii) terminate the lease and seek not only past damages, but damages for the loss of future rents (less any rent paid by a new tenant); (iii) seek to evict the tenant from possession but not terminate the lease, and to then seek past and future damages; or (iv) seek any combination of the above as well as any other damages allowed by law. In most states, if the landlord does not terminate the lease, or if they terminate the lease but seek damages for lost future rent, they have the responsibility to mitigate their damages by making a good faith attempt to re-let the Premises—though such re-letting will be under terms and conditions acceptable to the landlord. In such an event, however, the landlord's costs to re-let including broker's fees, tenant finish costs, and the like will be added to the old tenant's bill as additional damages.

- *Subordination.* This is a legal term that means the tenant's right to possession under the lease are junior to (thus "subordinate") to the superior rights of any lender to the landlord who has taken a security interest in the entire project. This means that the lender can take possession of the project, subject to the tenant's rights under the lease, should the landlord fail to pay on its loan. If this occurs, the tenant may be required to deliver the Rent directly to the lender, or may be asked to sign documents that recognize the lender's superior rights. Tenant's subordination does not mean that the tenant loses their rights under the lease. Instead, it means that upon notice, they will treat the lender as the "new" landlord.

- *Holding Over.* This is another legal term-of-art that refers to the tenant's continued possession of the Premises after the lease has expired or has been terminated. In most leases this covenant states that the tenant will hold the Premises only as a tenant from month-to-month at a Base Rent that may be anywhere from 125 percent to 200 percent greater than the Base Rent that was paid in the last month. Further, the Holdover covenant will provide for the termination of the tenancy after either party gives the other anywhere from one week to one month's written notice. This same covenant will also state that the entirety of the lease that is not otherwise amended, will remain in full force and effect.

Having said the above, some landlords do not provide for a Holdover. Instead, they declare that any continued possession after the expiration or termination is a separate breach of the lease for which additional damages will be assessed.

- *Covenant of Quiet Enjoyment.* Though this is usually found at the end of the lease, it is in fact one of the most important covenants for the tenant. Basically it provides that the tenant will be able to "enjoy" the use of the Premises without interference from the landlord or other tenants for so long as the tenant abides by the terms of the lease. It is this covenant that an injured tenant will point to if there is a violation of the lease by the landlord.

- *Estoppel Certificate.* An Estoppel Certificate is a letter or other written statement from the tenant that will set forth the tenant's perception of the current status of the lease. The Estoppel Certificate is usually required when the landlord is refinancing the entire project, though it can be requested for many other reasons. The Estoppel Certificate usually calls for: a statement of the name and contact information of the tenant and landlord; the identity of the Premises (such as "123 Street, Unit 6, Danville, Colorado, 80000"); the disclosure of the lease commencement date, expiration date, and any renewal options; the status of tenant's payment of Base Rent, Additional Rent, and the amount of the Security Deposit; a statement as to any defaults by the landlord under the lease; and other information.

- *Landlord's Interest.* Leases usually have a special covenant that states that the project itself is the only interest against which the tenant can collect any damages suffered. In other words, in the usual case, an injured party to a contract can collect against any asset that the breaching party may have. In the case of a lease, the only asset against which the tenant can collect is the project itself. Given that landlords usually mortgage a commercial property to the greatest extent possible, in practice, this covenant usually means that there is not a ready pile of cash available to pay a tenant for losses.

- *Additional Provisions.* Like any other contract, the lease will contain an Additional Provisions article that will cover such matters as the merger of prior agreements, oral or written, into the four corners of the current written lease, the manner by which written notice is to be delivered to a party, or the fact that there are rules and regulations that must be followed (understanding that such rules and regulations are usually attached to the lease).

Reading a lease is not for the faint at heart. It is filled with legalese and promises that are unfamiliar to someone not versed in lease intricacies.

The Best Location for Your New Business

It has been famously said that the three most important factors in the success of a business are *location, location, location.* This is an overstatement, of course, but it does point out how important it is to have a good location for certain types of businesses. Most retail and restaurant establishments rely on walk-by and drive-by traffic. You may have the best product or service in the world

You *must*, however, read and understand what is expected of you—and what you can expect from the landlord. Relying on your real estate lawyer or other real estate expert is essential to insure you get the deal you believe you negotiated.

and still fail if nobody can find you.

Your choice of a location for your business is critical and should be one area in which you focus a lot of research and evaluation to pick the absolute best site. Here are some things to keep in mind as you go through the site-selection process for your franchise:

> Download your Site Selection Checklist from www.franchisebiblestudy.com and follow it carefully to negotiate a great lease that is in your favor and save money and time.

- Don't expect your franchisor to do the work for you. They will ultimately approve the location, but you need to do the legwork and research.
- The franchisor may give you guidelines for the ideal site and intelligence from other franchise locations to assist you. If they don't have this information, try to find out the demographics of their most successful location and then mimic that information as best as possible.
- Choose a location that is best for your business, not one that is close to home. You would rather have a longer drive to a successful business than a short walk to a failing one.

Demographics and Location Analytics

In today's world you have more information at your fingertips than ever before. There are many tools and services that you can access to narrow the field of options and ultimately make your decision much easier. You will want to familiarize yourself with local demographics. This includes data such as a population's age, income, education, and other statistical information:

- Simple demographics are a good starting point but only the "tip of the iceberg" for the site-selection process.
- You can use a location analytics service to do an independent survey for the areas that you are considering that will provide more detailed information such as traffic count and nearby competition.
- Investing in this process is well worth it since a great location can be a huge factor in the success of your business.

Partially Equipped Locations

One money-saving tip when you are shopping sites is to look for partially equipped or built-out locations that may work for your business. For instance, you may be looking for a location for your new restaurant franchise and find a site that was a former restaurant. In this case, you may be able to save money since some of the existing infrastructure can be utilized, such as a hood system of grease trap. Here are some more tips:

- Make sure the location still meets all of the other criteria of a great location and resist jumping into a location just to save a little money. Try to figure out why the last restaurant failed—and learn from its mistakes.
- See if your franchisor allows partially equipped sites before you seek them out. Many franchisors require a completely new build-out and equipment package.

- Have the site inspected by professionals so you have a realistic idea of the actual cost savings. Include your architect, equipment supplier, lawyer, and engineer since each will evaluate the site from his or her professional perspective.

Tenant Improvement (TI) Dollars and Free Rent From the Landlord

Remember that the landlord has probably been in his or her business a long time and has negotiated leases with many tenants, brokers, and attorneys. It is very common for there to be an imbalance of knowledge between landlords and tenants that can result in future problems for the new business owner if they are not careful. This is very preventable if you take the right steps during your site-selection process.

> First and foremost, engage your attorney and financial professional to help you even the scales.

TI dollars is a definitive amount of money that the landlord may provide to a tenant that is to be used for the improvement of the space for the tenants use. Usually the amount is expressed as a certain dollar figure per square foot (for example: "$10.00 per square foot"—if you have a 1,000 square foot business, the landlord will reimburse you a total of $10,000) and is most often directed by the lease that it be used for build-out or construction items such as internal walls, bathrooms, or infrastructure systems like grease traps or ventilation.

Typically, you will be reimbursed by the landlord after you have completed your TI work and are open for business. Once you have delivered documentation to the landlord that: (i) proves that you have paid all of your bills (with copies of the bills attached; (ii) you have "lien waivers from all suppliers and workers that worked on the project; and (iii) you have received a "certificate of occupancy" (which comes from the city and county and which is the prerequisite to physically opening the doors for business), the landlord will cut the check.

You may also be able to negotiate free or discounted rent for a period of time.

Here are some big money-saving tips:

- Some landlords will give you a free rent provision in the form of a waived rental amount for a period of time so you can get up and running before you start paying.
- Have your commercial real estate broker prepare a *letter of intent* (LOI) stating exactly what you expect from the landlord and be sure that all monetary agreements are included in your final lease.
- Have the space evaluated before you commit so you know the actual status of the space and all related systems and structure.
- Most landlords prefer a longer lease commitment and will be willing to invest more TI dollars and free rent with a longer lease.

Choosing a Commercial Real Estate Broker

Not all brokers are created equal. Finding a quality broker who is committed to getting you the best location is very important. Remember, your business success potential is heavily impacted by your location:

- Interview a few commercial real estate brokers and choose the one that you feel will do the best job working for you.
- Check their references and ask if they were responsive and aggressive in the site search and negotiations with the landlord.
- The landlord usually has their own broker representing their side of the transaction, but in some cases may represent themselves.

Conclusion

Invest the time and resources necessary to find the ideal location for your new business. This is one decision that will impact your business immediately and can be very expensive and logistically difficult to change.

Make sure to conduct a thorough investigation when you are considering your business real estate decisions and get expert assistance to ensure the best possible scenario for your new business.

CHAPTER 6

Build-out and Construction Team

There are countless variables involved with the build-out and construction of a commercial location. Many businesses have suffered by cutting corners or trying to self-manage their own commercial projects. This chapter offers suggestions for assembling your construction team.

Choosing Your Project Manager

Project managers (PMs) serve as the lead on the project. They create the budget and timeline for every element of the construction from start to finish. The PM tracks progress on both a macro and micro level and makes sure that all steps take place in the correct order and on time.

> Interview and choose a project manager that has experience in your specific business category. This will enable you to view jobs that they have completed and talk to past clients.

The Gannt chart (see Figure 6-1), named after its inventor Henry L. Gannt, is a tool used by many project managers to manage the resources of a project and keep it moving forward on-time and on-budget. Make yourself familiar with your project's Gannt chart so you can also track progress.

Figure 6-1. Gannt Chart (Provided by MileStone Management)

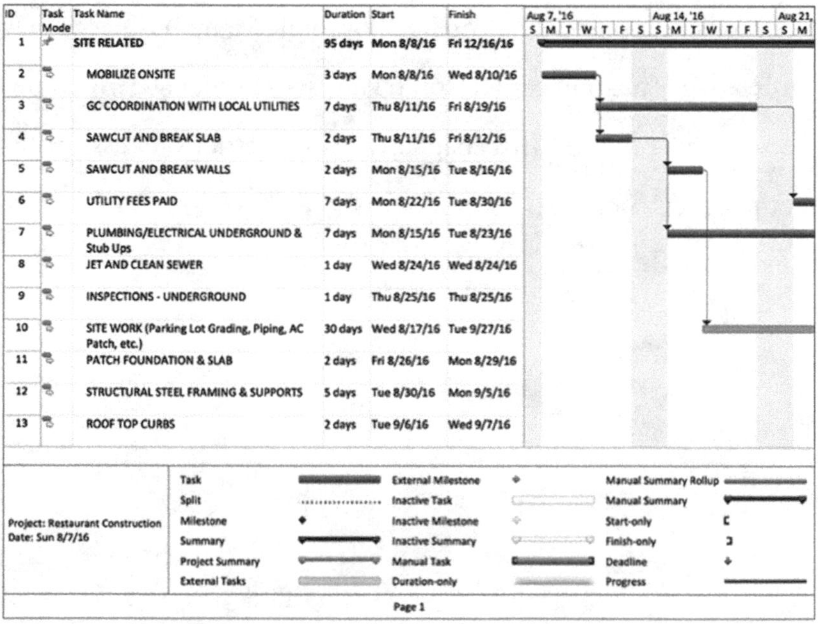

Choosing Your Architect

The architect will be in charge of the architectural drawings that act as the guide for the various trades to follow. Depending on the type of project, you may have multiple architects that specialize in different aspects of the project, such as a kitchen architect.

You may find referrals for the architects from the franchisor, project manager, or general contractors. Be sure to adequately research each before hiring. Remember, though, at the end of the day, you are the one writing the checks and need to be in charge.

Choosing Your General Contractor

The *general contractor* (GC) is the lead contractor on the job and is in charge of the *sub-contractors* (subs). These subs include framers, electricians, plumbers, Heating Ventilation Air Conditioning (HVAC) contractors, and other tradespeople. The GC will usually be responsible for hiring, scheduling, and paying the subs. The GC will have the oversight of the PM. The GC often assumes the role of PM on projects that do not have one.

Dealing with Permits and Inspections

Your site will be subject to building permits and inspection requirements. These will vary in scope, time, and expense, depending on your location and the associated governing agencies.

Your construction team should be experienced in this process for your area and will factor this in to the project budget and timeline. It is important to make sure that your project manager stays on top of this process so the project does not stall while waiting on a permit or inspection approval, which can cost you money every day that the job is stopped.

Build-Out Budget and Timeline

Your franchisor may provide you with detailed lists of required equipment, materials, and supplies for your location. They may also provide a floor plan and other information but it is still up to you and your local team to manage the build-out of your site. Between the information that your franchisor provides and the data that you and your construction team assemble, you should be able to structure a comprehensive project budget and timeline.

Franchisor Requirements

Franchisor requirements will vary from one to the next. Some franchisors have very strict processes and deliver a "business in a box" to the job site that includes everything to build and open the franchised store. In this case, you may request a "vanilla shell" from the landlord, which is a basic space that is ready for build-out. The franchisor may even provide the entire construction team and deliver the store to you complete and ready to open.

Other franchisors have less control and assistance, leaving more in your hands. Your level of responsibility depends on the franchise you are joining and the related requirements. These requirements should be spelled out in their franchise disclosure documents. Your franchisor should be willing to discuss their process with you so you can establish a clear strategy to reach your goals.

Conclusion

Choosing the best build-out and construction team is a critical step as you prepare to launch your new franchise. Now that you used this section to successfully navigate the tangible creation of your new location, you can begin the process of building your winning team to help you run the place.

CHAPTER 7

Building a Winning Team

At this stage of your franchise roadmap, you have completed a lot of the hard work. The stage is set, and now it is time to build your winning team. The people you choose will be trusted with your investment and future when they come to work. Use this section to recruit, nurture, and incentivize your employees and thrive.

Recruiting Applicants

The first step is to create a staffing plan to identify the type and number of positions. You can then render job descriptions for each position. This will help you with the interviewing process as well as the training. Your franchisor may provide assistance with this and give you training and guidelines to follow in the franchise operations manual for the best places to seek applicants.

Regardless of the positions that you are hiring for, it is advisable to adopt a consistent interviewing and hiring procedure for your business. This will make the ongoing staffing process easier for you and your employees to follow:

- Have interested parties meet with you in-person for the interview.
- Are applicants on time and dressed properly?
- First impressions do matter. If you are not impressed on the first visit, it probably won't get better moving forward.
- Are they enthusiastic about the opportunity?
- Did they research your business on and offline before the interview to prepare?
- Your franchisor may offer assistance and guidelines for hiring and interviewing employees.

Keeping Good Records and HR Support

Good employee records offer you an added insurance policy as well as efficient records. You will want to keep an employee file for each staff member. You can begin with his or her application and/or resume and then add other documents such as:

- *Customer feedback.* Surveys, emails, notes, and transcripts of calls. Positive and negative comments should be noted in the file.
- *Performance reviews.* Periodic performance reviews help with direction and growth.
- *Write-ups.* This is usually a note written by a manager or owner, to keep a record of positive and negative occurrences.

- *Training documents.* Certifications test scores, tracking, and goals.
- *Termination records and exit review.*

Compensation, Bonuses, Benefits, and Incentives

Many franchisors will provide guidelines for you to follow, but it is up to you as the business owner to apply the systems provided to hire and build a thriving team. This is an important element of your business success plan.

Compensation is one of the main items that prospective employees focus on when they consider a new position. Statistics have also shown that other factors are important, including a feeling of purpose and belonging, which you will build into your company culture. You can factor your pay scale into your job descriptions as you develop them using comparable pay rates in your area.

Bonuses are a tried-and-true method of tying employee performance to their income. Bonus structures can be designed in many ways such as customer service programs or the achievement of financial goals. The most successful bonuses usually enable the individual to earn the bonus based on their performance.

Benefits for your employees can offer them extra incentive to stay with your company for the long-term. Employee benefits can range from very basic to more extravagant:

- Discounts on products or services of the company
- Free or discounted food and beverages for food service businesses
- Health insurance
- Matching 401(k) plan
- Profit sharing
- Stock options

Disciplinary Actions and Termination

Employee management includes both incentives and disciplinary elements. The old saying "slow to hire and quick to fire" is a common rule of thumb. Much like parenting, a business owner has to be able to maintain order by enforcing the rules and policies of the organization. It is a good idea to consult with your local labor division and read up on employee laws, especially if you are a first-time employer. The best practice is to always keep good records of any disciplinary actions or terminations that you or your managers execute.

Legal Considerations

Legal issues should be a rare occurrence if you operate a safe and professional work environment. You may want to consult with a labor attorney to familiarize yourself with possible areas of exposure. Your local labor division will also have resources available. Some of the common areas of exposure to learn about are:

- Discrimination
- Sexual harassment
- Wrongful termination
- Failure to pay

Payroll and Payroll Tax Management

Managing your payroll and payroll taxes is a very important responsibility of every business owner who has employees. Payroll can be pretty tricky if you do not have a strong accounting background, so hiring a professional payroll service is advisable. These services are affordable and also help you with payroll tax processing and reporting.

Company Culture and Managing Staff

Your company culture is something that you create that nobody else can do for you. *Culture* is the core belief system that drives your business. This includes the relationships that you have with your employees, customers, and community. Your culture will also reflect your management style, commitment to customer service, and professionalism. It is the way people feel when they interact with your business.

Managing your staff can take on a variety of forms. It has been said that you *manage* things and *lead* people. This is one area where you can invest more time and resources to improve over time.

> Be proactive in creating a positive company culture from the very beginning of your new business. Create an inviting atmosphere and encourage people to give you feedback as you develop your business.

Your leadership skills will determine the direction of your company, especially with business models that require a large employee team. Your franchisor may offer training and support in this area. You can also find many resources online and through local libraries and business schools to further your education.

Conclusion

Building your winning team is an important element of your businesses growth. Apply the concepts in this chapter to create good habits from the very beginning. You can find more resources at www.entrepreneur.com/franchiseresources.

CHAPTER 8

Launch, Grow, Thrive!

Now the stage is set for your franchise success story. Your business journey has brought you to the point where you have your franchise ready to launch, grow, and thrive. Apply the tips in this chapter to make the most of your opportunity.

Marketing Your Franchise

Your franchisor will provide you with training and support, including the marketing of your new business. As the franchise owner, it is your responsibility to apply the marketing tools and techniques to build your business. Marketing is one area of your business that you can always learn more about. There are many resources on and offline to increase your proficiency:

- Apply all of the tools that the franchisor provides. You've invested a lot, so make the most of the resources and guidance that they offer.
- Understand that even though the franchisor is there to assist you, it is up to you to market and grow your business.
- Create and apply a comprehensive marketing plan that includes all of the six pillar categories from Chapter 1.

Making the Most of Your Franchise

You invest a lot of money and time when you purchase a franchise. Surprisingly, many franchise owners choose not to apply what they've paid for. The franchisor has created a system for the franchise owners to follow and have made the costly mistakes so you don't have to.

> Historically, the most successful franchisees are the ones that more closely follow the franchise system.

GROWING AND ADDING MORE UNITS

Some of the most successful business owners are multi-unit franchise owners. It doesn't take long for a successful franchisee to determine that if one franchise works, two is twice as good. Many franchisors will offer incentives for franchise owners that want to add more units since they are already up and running and will need less training and support.

STRIVE TO BECOME THE "TOP PRODUCER"

Franchise organizations that are run well understand that building the franchise community is a critical strategy for large growth. These franchisors may have friendly competitions and award top producing franchise owners. Strive to be your company's top producing owner, and you will win on all fronts.

HELP YOUR FRANCHISOR GROW

The key to success with any franchise organization is a foundation that creates a win, win, win, and win. When everyone works together, and looks out for each other, you will see that the franchisor, franchisees, customers, and employees all win! The give-more-than-you-receive philosophy can really pay off. Franchise owners that contribute to the overall effort of the franchise organization may also find growth opportunities as the company grows.

BECOME A GREAT VALIDATOR

The validation that you receive from existing franchise owners is a big part of your decision-making process when you are shopping for the right franchise. You probably talked to franchisees before you made your decision to buy your franchise. Due to the fact that this is a huge part of growing a successful franchise organization, it is in everyone's best interest to spend the time necessary to answer questions when prospective franchisees call you for validation.

> Not happy? Be proactive and let your franchisor know if you are not satisfied. This gives them the opportunity to remedy the situation. A bad review when a validation call comes in hurts the effort of the whole company, which ultimately hurts your business too.

Owner's Advisory Committee

Many franchise organizations will organize an *owner's advisory committee* or *council* (sometimes referred to as the OAC). This is a strategy to facilitate communication and participation between the franchisor's corporate team and the franchise community. Participating on the OAC gives you a voice, and even though most are advisory only, you can influence the direction of the company.

Leadership Opportunities

As you grow with the franchisor, you may find a variety of leadership opportunities. These may take the form of the OAC, training, mentorships, or speaking/coaching at corporate conventions and events. These opportunities can be very lucrative and may open doors for you. Be sure to balance your time with your franchise business to keep your core business thriving if you pursue these opportunities.

Building Your Enterprise and Legacy

Investor portfolios have changed quite a bit over the recent years as other traditional investment options have struggled. Many entrepreneurs are investing in themselves and building a business portfolio vs. a stock portfolio to have more control of the outcome. Franchising is a perfect business model for this type of strategy due to the flexible options and the "duplicable" nature, which enables you to grow faster and more efficiently.

MULTI-UNIT OWNERSHIP

Your business portfolio can grow by first becoming a multi-unit franchise owner. Once you get the hang of your franchise, adding one or more units can make a lot of sense. Consider the following facts:

- If you make money with one unit, you should be able to make more by adding units.
- Banks are far more interested in lending money to operators that have a proven track record.
- Your franchisor built a system of duplication in order to franchise across the country. You can use this same infrastructure on a smaller level to grow your network of franchised units.
- Your franchisor may offer you incentives to add units since you are already successful within their franchise organization and will

grow faster with less strain on their training and support staff.

Structure Options within Franchising to Consider

The franchising business structure offers several options within the expansion model. This section describes the different options and applications for each type.

SINGLE UNIT

The most common option is the single-unit franchise. This is simply one individual or business entity purchasing one franchised unit. In many cases, a single-unit franchisee will open more units down the road once they acquire more experience, revenue, and confidence that they can replicate their success. Since the franchise model is built to be duplicated, it lends itself to owner level expansion.

MULTI-UNIT

The multi-unit franchise buyer is usually an individual or business entity that contracts to purchase multiple franchise locations at the same time. Many franchisors require that prospects start by opening and growing one unit for a period of time before they are permitted to open more units.

AREA DEVELOPER

An *area developer* is an individual or business entity that signs an agreement to open a predetermined number of franchised units over a mutually agreed-upon timeline. The same entity owns all of the units but is given a period of time to open all of the units.

The area developer will usually sign an *area developer agreement* (ADA) as well as the corresponding franchise agreement(s). This strategy can enable you to secure the territory that best fits your long-term goals. You must have the appropriate infrastructure and financial capabilities for this model and only execute an ADA if you can follow through with all of the obligations.

You may lose certain rights as well as money in the event that you are unable to perform under the agreements.

REGIONAL DEVELOPER

A *regional developer* (RD, sometimes mistakenly referred to as a *master franchise*) is a hybrid between an area developer and a master franchise. The RD will usually sign a regional developer agreement as well as the corresponding franchise agreement(s).

The RD is an individual or business entity that usually runs their own franchise(s) as well as taking on some of the recruiting and support responsibilities of the franchisor in a region in exchange for a revenue share. In most cases the revenue share with the franchisor will include a percentage of the *initial franchise fees* (IFFs) collected from franchises sold in the regional developer's region in the event that they were involved with the recruiting and/or onboarding process.

The RD may also share in the royalty stream of the respective franchisees in their region if agreed upon by their franchisor. This percentage is relative to the level of support and training that they provide to their regional franchise community.

The franchisor may see this option as a good way to spread out the recruiting, support, and training aspects of the business. This can be a very lucrative opportunity due to the fact that you can "piggyback" on the infrastructure that the franchisor has invested a lot of time and money to build. This is a benefit for the franchisor as well if it is a good fit for all parties.

MASTER FRANCHISE

The term *master franchise* is often confused with the aforementioned area developer or regional developer models. A true master franchise is usually an individual or business entity that wants to own and operate a franchised organization in a different market than that of the franchisor. The master franchisee will take on the role of the franchisor in their assigned region. The master franchisee will usually sign a *master franchise agreement* (MFA) with the franchisor. This is usually a good model for global expansion of a franchise organization. The master franchisee will need to comply with all applicable franchise and business laws within their country or region as well as agreements with the franchisor.

Military Veteran Resources

Many military franchise owners have reported that one of the challenges of moving from the military life to that of civilian life is the loss of their community as well as the focus of the mission at hand. Veteran franchisees have been historically successful at running franchises and following the structured systems to grow their businesses. If you are a military veteran, seek a franchisor that has a true company culture of community as well as a work structure that fits your style. The franchise organization that you belong to can be an awesome extended family as you grow your business.

Conclusion

Take advantage of all of the opportunities that are available to you. The franchise model is the most successful business expansion method in our history due to the common effort of many to build a common business success story.

PART II

Franchise Your Business

(Becoming a Franchisor)

Go to www.franchisebiblestudy.com and download the Franchise Your Business Roadmap to guide you through the chapters in this part. You can also find additional resources at www.entrepreneur.com/franchiseresources.

CHAPTER 9

Franchise Fundamentals

Many well-organized company programs that are short on expansion capital have turned into efficient, highly profitable networks of franchised outlets. The desired end result of this popular business system called *franchising* is a highly motivated, cost-cutting, quality-conscious retailer who provides a product or service to the customer. This method of operation can be far more efficient and profitable than a company-owned enterprise, which may be operated by high-priced and/or disinterested company employees.

Franchising, simply put, is a means of expanding a business operation by licensing a third party to engage in a franchise system under a required marketing plan or system using a common trademark, service mark, or trade name (Marks) for a fee. Franchising is available to businesses distributing both products and services and to those distributing services only.

Starting a Whole New Business

One of the basic things to understand for a new franchisor is the reality that franchising is the launching of a whole new business. Many have "tried franchising" or added it on as a side business, only to fail. You will want to fully investigate the franchise process to determine your ability and commitment level before you invest time and money. You can certainly start small and grow your infrastructure as your franchise community grows, but the new franchise organization will need to be managed.

Business Expansion Options

This section discusses the various methods used to expand a business. Before you move into the franchise world, it is a good idea to evaluate all of the options.

CHAIN OUTLETS

A *chain* is a group of business outlets that are duplicated in various markets by the same individual or entity. This model can be expensive and challenging to manage since all outlets are operated and funded by the original owner/entity. Large chain models usually have large operational budgets and enable the highest level of control.

This model applies to owner/entities that have large operational and growth budgets and desire to control all of the daily management of the units.

BUSINESS OPPORTUNITY

In a business opportunity setting, the *purchaser* is specifically prohibited from using the *seller's* trademarks. The lack of this element removes the business opportunity from federal franchise regulation and usually from franchise regulation by the states.

The federal definition of a "business opportunity" is found at 16 C.F.R. 437 et seq., and contains the following paraphrased requirements: (a) the seller solicits a prospective purchaser to enter into a new business; (b) the prospective purchaser makes a required payment; and (c) the seller represents to the purchaser that seller will: (i) provide locations to the purchaser for the use or operation of the equipment or services sold to purchaser; *or* (ii) provide outlets, accounts, or customers (including internet access) to the purchaser and to whom the purchaser may sell the goods or services; *or* (iii) buy back from the purchaser any of the goods or services that purchaser creates in the business.

This model applies to owner/entities that want to expand and collect fees from others that want to purchase, own, and operate a business system that is offered by the owner/entity but operate under a different trade name and with very little support and infrastructure.

LICENSING

The definition of a *license* is the grant to the Licensee (person or entity granted the right to use the trademark) of the right to use the Licensor's (owner of the trademark) trademark, for a fee, and which use is subject to the Licensor's "control" over the goods or services sold under the license. There are three pillars: (a) Licensor's grant to the Licensee of the right to use Licensor's trademark; (b) for a fee; (c) and Licensor exerts some direction and control over Licensee's use of the trademark.

This model applies to owner/entities that want to expand and collect fees from others that want to purchase, own and operate a business system offered by the owner/entity and operate under their trademark(s). The licensing model has less control and support from the owner/entity than a franchise model.

FRANCHISING

The definition of a *franchise* (taken from the federal definition of a franchise—16 Code of Federal Regulation 436 et seq.) and paraphrased here is: (a) "franchisor's" (owner of the trademark) grant to franchisee (person or entity granted the right to use the trademark) of the right to use franchisor's trademark; (b) for a fee; (c) and franchisor exerts a "significant degree of control over the franchisee's method of operation," *or* "provides significant assistance in the franchisee's method of operation."

This model applies to owner/entities that want to start a whole new business and grow a larger equity building business asset. A franchisor can expand and collect fees from others that want to purchase, own, and operate a franchised business system that is offered by the owner/entity and operate under their trademark(s), business systems, training, and ongoing support. Franchise buyers will typically pay a substantial "up front" *initial franchise fee* (IFF) as well as ongoing royalties and other fees. Royalties usually are a percentage (4–6 percent) of each franchise owner's monthly gross revenue. These ongoing fees enable the franchisor to continuously improve the business systems and support the franchise community to help them grow their respective businesses.

Structure Options within Franchising

One of the advantages of the franchise model is its flexible structure options. These options offer growth benefits to both the franchisor and the franchise owners. We've covered the definitions of the four primary options. This section will give you some considerations for each.

SINGLE-UNIT FRANCHISE

The single-unit franchise is the most common model, where the franchise buyer profile is usually made up of individuals or families that desire business ownership. Some franchise organizations suffer by trying to limit the buyers to only multi-unit ownership, which can overburden the buyers, resulting in failure.

MULTI-UNIT FRANCHISE

The good news is that many successful single-unit operators choose to become multi-unit owners. They learn that the success with one franchise unit can be duplicated to expand and achieve their goals by utilizing the infrastructure built by the franchisor. You will want to make sure that interested franchise owners are vetted by your internal franchise-development team. Even though they are existing franchisees, they need to be qualified for multi-unit ownership. One good franchise is much better than two struggling franchises, so be sure that they can handle the added expense and management duties.

> Your multi-unit franchisees will take less training and support than a brand new franchise owner, so you may consider offering incentives for them to add units such as reduced franchise fees.

AREA DEVELOPERS

Franchisees that have the desire, ability, and wherewithal to build a faster network of franchised units may consider signing an *area developer agreement* (ADA). This option can enable faster growth as long as all parties follow through with the terms. Committing a franchisee to an ADA who isn't fully capable can be a recipe for disaster.

REGIONAL DEVELOPERS

The *regional developer* (RD) model can be very lucrative for both the franchisor as well as the RDs. This model shares the responsibilities and rewards so both parties have an incentive to grow the region. A common franchisor mistake is awarding *regional developer agreements* (RDAs) to unqualified parties hoping that this will reduce their responsibility for an area or region by shifting that to the RD. Many RDs fail, which hurts the whole system. It is a good idea to have prospective RDs own and operate a single unit or multi-unit franchise for a period of time before you approve them for an RDA.

Advantages and Disadvantages of Franchising

It is important to consider the pros and cons of franchising your business before you commit your time and resources. Franchising can be a great way to expand your business, but it is a big decision, and you will only succeed with a 100 percent focused effort.

ADVANTAGES OF FRANCHISING

When discussing the advantages of franchising for the franchisor, it is inevitable to discuss the advantages available to the franchisee as well. This is because many advantages for one are also considered advantages for the other. So, even though the following list specifies the advantages to the franchisor or the franchisee, most are generally held to be advantages for both:

- There is potential for rapid expansion with minimum capital expenditures.
- Direct managing responsibilities become the franchisee's obligation and allow the franchisor more freedom to do other things.
- The franchisee generally has pride of ownership and self-motivation because of his or her capital investment and stake in future profits. (This self-motivation generally results in the franchisee's lowering his or her costs, resulting in higher profit margins for the franchisee and greater consumer markets for the franchisor than normally attainable by company employees.)
- A franchisee will generally have a minimum number of line-management employees and a greater number of staff advisory employees.
- National and local advertising dollars are available for franchisees in far greater amounts than could be generated by the franchisor or franchisee alone.
- There is increased buying power, resulting in lower possible purchase prices for goods used by the franchisee.
- Research and development facilities are available to the franchisor through reports from franchisees.
- The franchisor can have a steady cash flow from royalties.
- The franchisor can maintain consistency and quality in its franchises through wise and fair franchise contract provisions.
- Some limits of liability extend to the final consumer. (Franchisees generally are not held to be agents of the franchisor in the event of injuries due to the franchisee's negligence, as opposed to liability

that extends to a company for injuries suffered in a branch store based on company employee negligence.)

Other advantages a franchisor may enjoy can be directly attributed to the advantages that a franchisee will enjoy. In short, if the franchisee is happy, the franchisor will be happy. For more on franchisee advantages, refer to Chapter 1.

DISADVANTAGES OF FRANCHISING

Of course, as is the case with most things in life, there is usually a downside to every decision you make or every venture you pursue. And when it comes to franchising, you need to be aware of some of the disadvantages. This section will help you be better informed and more prepared in making your franchising decision:

- *Decreased net receipts.* You will make less than that of a company-owned store since you will only collect a royalty, which is a small percentage of the unit revenue.
- *Independence of franchisees.* The franchise owners are not your employees, and you do not have direct management control.
- *Difference in required business skills.* You may have a different management style than the franchise owners.
- *Costs can be high.* The upfront investment to franchise your business can be substantial.

Can Your Business Be Franchised?

If you have a successful business that is susceptible to a regional or national system of marketing and you do not want to share control or risk the personality conflicts that come with bringing in investors who would become your equals in making business decisions, then franchising may be your best course of action. To help you determine whether your business could be franchised, review some of the qualifiers and considerations described below.

ARE YOU FRANCHISOR MATERIAL?

Before you evaluate your business as a potential franchise, be sure to evaluate yourself as a potential franchisor. Often, a person who might successfully operate a business that is susceptible to franchising may not be cut out to be a franchisor. Consider your qualities and remember that franchising is more than the business of selling services and/or products to a consumer. In addition, as a franchisor, you will be an educator, trainer, psychologist, minister, and perpetual hand-holder to your franchisees. You will also be a fee collector, extracting an initial fee for the franchisee to begin business and then collecting royalties for the life of the franchise.

You will need to be aware of the franchisee-franchisor relationship and always remember to allow your individual franchisees the flexibility to manage their own businesses. Always treat them as independent business owners, not employees. It is important you carefully set forth the guidelines of this independent contractor relationship in the initial contract, the disclosure document, and all further communications to franchisees.

IS THERE A MARKET FOR YOUR PARTICULAR PRODUCT OR SERVICE?

Do not consider franchising your business unless you have a known, local market for your product or service. Marketability is determined by need, and need is determined by competition.

For example, if you are running a hamburger stand, your chances of finding a market for your franchise and a market for your franchisees are relatively small in today's business community. However, if you have a unique way of running a hamburger stand, it is entirely possible to franchise it. Take the Wendy's operation, for example, which gained steam by introducing the system of in-line preparation of hamburgers as the consumer watches and waits for his or her order. This is in contrast with the traditional method of preparing fast-food hamburgers out of view and then setting them on a warming tray until someone places an order. Wendy's catered to consumers who wanted to see their hamburgers made to order right before their eyes.

Demand is the crucial force here. It is just as important as uniqueness. Your unique product or service must be desired not only by the people who want to buy franchises from you, but also by the people who will buy products or services from the franchisees.

WHAT MARKET RESEARCH MUST YOU DO?

If your product or service is relatively new and not extensively offered by anyone else, but has proven to be in demand, your first task is to determine those sections of the country that would most likely buy your products or services, based on needs similar to those of your present customers. For example, a new type of thermal underwear would not go over well with residents of California's Palm Springs area; however, a successful gas-saving device might take hold anywhere in the world.

If your product or service is not relatively new, you can retain market research firms to prepare extensive reports concerning the types of consumers in various regions and their needs and buying power. This could be rather expensive, so an alternative is to do your own research by visiting the reference department of your local library and by searching on the internet. You can study the yellow pages of phone books of the various cities in which you would like to offer your product or service to determine if any competition exists in those areas. You can also conduct an internet search and review online business directories and business review sites (such as *Yelp!*) to get information on potential competitors.

You will also want to interview existing franchisors and franchisees for their insights on franchising. People like telling others of their business accomplishments, so this should be a particularly enjoyable aspect of researching the franchising potential of your business.

Government agencies are also very helpful in providing demographic information and market research data. In particular, the U.S. Department of Commerce (www.commerce.gov), Bureau of Economic Analysis (www.bea.gov), and the U.S. Department of Labor, Bureau of Labor Statistics (www.bls.gov) have conducted extensive studies on the regional consumer habits of Americans. Search for "consumer habits" on these government websites, and you can obtain useful data for your research.

It is always necessary to do an initial study of the existing demand for the products or services you are thinking of offering through a franchise system. A more extensive study can be conducted by potential franchisees. If you feel an initial market is out there, utilize potential franchisees by encouraging them to make their own market study as a prerequisite to receiving a license from you.

The Final Decision to Franchise

Before you make your final decision to franchise, you need to know the following:

- You have what it takes to be a franchisor.
- Your product is unique and in demand, and your business is profitable and promising to prospective franchisees.
- You have a market for your product or service.
- Your service or product is associated with a trademark that is, or can be, registered.

In addition, you have probably already decided you do not want to share your control with any investors in the form of partners or shareholders and you have investigated other business expansion alternatives. You should also have a strong idea of what to look for in your future franchisees.

Before you launch your plan to expand by franchising, prepare a thorough business plan so you can realistically look at the financial outlay each new outlet will require to get up and running. Then compare that with the revenue you can expect to receive from fees, royalties, and sales of ingredients and services. Some of the costs specific to franchising that you will want to include in your business plan are overhead costs of your franchise operation, such as salaries and benefits for yourself and employees in your head office and trainers and sales staff, as well as normal office expenses like rent, office equipment, car allowances, and travel. Plan in the cost of finding franchisees. This could include buying ads, traveling to franchise shows, preparing brochures and videos, and entertaining. In addition, add a healthy allowance for startup and ongoing legal, accounting, and advertising fees.

Be overly conservative as you project the timing and amount of income you expect to receive from your franchise outlets. You will have determined the mixture of franchise fees, royalties, and product sales that will bring you income from your franchisees. Pad your expectations of how soon these revenues will flow back to you, instead of basing your predictions solely on how your business worked in the past.

Another important factor you should investigate before making your franchise decision is the advantages and disadvantages of each legal form of business organization—sole proprietorship, partnership, or corporation. If you form either a sole proprietorship or a partnership, your operation will be subject to unlimited liability: If the business fails and its debts exceed its assets, the sole proprietor or the partners can be held individually liable for unpaid debts. Because of this liability issue, most franchisors choose a corporate entity, in order to limit their liabilities to the assets of the corporation. Refer to Chapter 3 for more on the advantages and disadvantages of different types of business entities. To find out more on legal forms of business organization, especially incorporating, consult an attorney and a certified public accountant.

Working Capital Considerations

The costs involved in franchising will vary according to geographic areas, expansion time, and availability of potential franchisees, as well as the complexity of the product or service being sold.

A small, one-person operation that has a profitable product or service with controlled lower costs and an ever-increasing market can franchise just as well as a larger competitor, provided the small business offers consistent services or products or both to its franchisees in a manner that will motivate the franchisees to remain in the franchise family. This usually means that the franchisor either performs a service or provides a product to the franchisee that the franchisee cannot obtain elsewhere or offers the product or service to the franchisee at a price lower than any price the franchisee could secure elsewhere or at a quality unavailable anywhere else.

This is necessary at least until the franchisor's trademark attains the recognition that will automatically generate continuing business for the franchisee or until the common franchisee advertising fund grows big enough to enhance the franchisee's business through customer recognition.

As a would-be franchisor, you must have a "glue" or "hold" on the franchisee that will be strong enough to keep the franchisee interested in remaining a licensed franchisee. In addition to providing the franchisee with products at lower prices and of the best available quality, as described earlier, such additional holds include supporting the franchisee's success. To demonstrate such ongoing support, you can provide continued training sessions, co-op advertising, billing and accounting services, discounted inventory prices from third-party suppliers, and exclusive product distribution.

The amount of working capital you need to start a franchise operation will vary depending on your size, rate of expansion, complexity of training, necessity of site selection and architectural planning, extent of marketing, attractiveness of the franchise, the capital investment required from franchisees, and other factors.

Carefully planned, slow expansion by a franchisor with a small, but efficient franchise-oriented staff or consultants and a product or service attractive to potential franchisees can be capitalized for under $100,000 by utilizing the existing franchise-trained staff.

> Realistic financial forecasts and iron-clad budgets, including necessary ongoing support systems for the franchisees, are the keys to successful franchise endeavors.

Do not franchise your business without first developing a well-thought-out business plan. In this plan, you should set forth realistic marketing goals along with expansion plans, advertising programs, capital outlay, and projected costs for a five-year period. Make sure you have sufficient resources available. Don't rely on initial franchise fees and royalties to support you in the first few years of your business.

Conclusion

At this point you should have a pretty good idea of whether or not you want to move forward to franchise your business. Building your successful franchise organization can be very exciting and rewarding. Your company can create countless jobs and enable families to thrive. Note your progress on your franchise roadmap (www.franchisebiblestudy.com) and move to the next chapter.

CHAPTER 10

Franchise Law Considerations

Many successful business owners decide to expand their businesses through distributorships, licenses, or joint venture/ partnership arrangements to distribute and sell their products or services and, as a result, save themselves a considerable amount of capital investment in building or leasing company-owned outlets. These third-party arrangements—whether they are called distributorships, license agreements, partnerships, or joint ventures—all have one thing in common: They may violate federal and state franchise laws, depending on the nature and terms of the relationship.

These industrious and sincere business owners, in their desire to adopt a successful marketing system and expand their businesses, may very well be entering into a nightmare of litigation and government agency investigations, resulting in considerable civil damages and government penalties. In most cases, the business owner is unaware of the impending danger and perhaps has even consulted an attorney not experienced in or aware of the ramifications of federal and state franchise and business opportunity laws.

It is entirely possible that an entrepreneur may purchase, or an uninformed business owner may market, a company that is engaged in franchising without being registered under applicable state law or without following the appropriate directives set forth in federal law.

A typical example of this is the business owner who has developed a new or improved product or service and has experienced a certain degree of success in marketing it. He or she must now decide whether or not to raise and risk additional capital to provide more marketing outlets for the expanding line of products or services, which would include hiring people to conduct his or her business in these new locations. All of this takes a considerable amount of time and money. In most cases, the money is unavailable, interest rates are prohibitive, or it is almost impossible to find additional competent employees to market the product or service properly. The business owner then decides that he or she will teach others to market the product or service and charge them for his or her expertise. The recipients of this training will, of course, want the right to use the name of the business owner, which, in almost all instances, is an integral part of the sales success of the product or service. The business owner, by the same token, will want to exert some type of control or limitations on the use of his or her name by third parties, so that it can be used only under certain controlled circumstances, avoiding any chance of bringing the name into disrepute.

If any of these restrictions is violated, the business owner will want to call off the deal and revoke the right to use the trademark. In addition, in order for the fledgling business to succeed financially, it will be necessary for the business owner to teach the third-party licensee, distributor, or joint venture methods of marketing the product or service that will bring a degree of success to the third party's operation. This marketing plan or scheme will be such as to correspond to the methods used by the business owner in gaining his or her initial success.

The end result desired by both the third party and the business owner is to maintain an operation engaged in marketing a product or a service that will look to the public as if it is one big organization with a single identity and universal continuity of service. The business owner, of course, is going to want some type of remuneration for training the third party and allowing him or her to become part of what looks like a "big happy family." The consideration is usually in the form of an initial fee to cover the training and, in many cases, a percentage of future gross profits. In some cases it may be the outright sale of a facility and the right to use the name for a one-lump-sum payment. Such an arrangement is clearly a franchise under federal and state franchise law.

The legal reality of the situation—that this is a franchise—is even less apparent to the business owner who is selling a product rather than a service, such as an image-engraving system or coin-stamping equipment, to a third party.

Franchise Discloser Document and Franchise Agreement

The Federal Trade Commission (FTC) requires that all companies that offer franchises in the United States adhere to the FTC regulations. Chapter 3 details the franchise disclosure document and franchise agreement, and a sample is included online at www.entrepreneur.com/franchiseresources. Here are some items to factor in as you develop your franchise documents:

- Hire a qualified franchise attorney to write your documents. Franchising is a very intricate specialty and you do not want to risk this step by doing it yourself or using an attorney that does not have a franchise practice.
- Set up a system for tracking the distribution of the franchise

documents to ensure that the state-appropriate docs are sent to the correct states.

- Create a tracking system that notes the distribution dates and receipts for all franchise documents.
- Implement systems to track compliance items within the franchise documents, such as annual financial reports and insurance certificates.
- Allowing compliance items to go by the wayside can reduce the durability of your contracts.
- Map out the registration states and create a strategy and budget for moving into those states as needed.

The disclosure document required by the applicable state governments typically must contain, among other things, the following information:

- Background information regarding the franchisor, predecessors, and affiliates
- The identity and business experience of key personnel
- Pending franchisor litigation
- Prior franchisor bankruptcies
- Details of franchise fees and other fees
- An outline of the franchisee's initial investment
- Franchisor's assistance and related obligations of both the franchisor and franchisee
- Territory
- Trademarks
- Patents, copyrights, and proprietary information
- Obligations of the franchisee to participate in the actual operation of the franchised business
- Restrictions on what the franchisee may sell
- Renewal, termination, transfer, and dispute resolution
- Arrangements with public figures
- Financial performance representations

- Outlets and franchisee information
- Financial statements of the franchisor

In addition, a copy of the franchise agreement and an explanation of its more pertinent provisions are also required. Many of these topics are discussed in greater detail in Chapters 1 and 3 and online at www.franchise biblestudy.com

In most cases, if you are in a registration state, you will submit your application with the franchise agreement and disclosure document to a state official, who will then determine whether or not it has met the requirements of the state law and advise you accordingly. These state statutes, like the federal statute, require a complete disclosure of certain enumerated items. The states do not determine whether or not the statements in the disclosure document are true or false, but, in the event that a stated item is not true, the state gives the franchisee an additional legal right for damages.

In some cases, a violation may result in administrative or criminal sanctions or both, in addition to the civil remedies afforded to the franchisee. States that have franchise investment laws have statutes that can be used in seeking damages through the courts or arbitration for both loss of profit and return of monies spent in the event that a franchisor violates these laws. This is in addition to remedies for fraud that are available to any victimized business owner.

In addition, the states with franchise registration laws, and the FTC under its rules on franchising, have given government authorities certain powers to seek criminal remedies against franchisors violating the franchise acts and, in some instances, the power to order the franchisor to pay back franchise fees received in violation of the acts.

If you insist upon doing your own disclosure documents—which franchise experts do not recommend—you should familiarize yourself with the laws of the state in which you intend to franchise. At the very least, contact the various state agencies to see whether you are required to comply with their laws if you are selling to a franchisee residing in that state or if you want to operate franchises in that state.

In all states with franchise registration laws, if the prospective franchisee is a resident of the state and the franchise is to be operated in that state, the franchise laws of that state will apply. Also remember that you can make no claims regarding existing franchisees' earnings or potential earnings unless you provide an earnings claim document. Those states with franchise registration laws also require an approved earnings claim document.

Federal Law

The federal government entered into regulating franchises on October 21, 1979, when the Federal Trade Commission (FTC) published its first original interpretive guides to the agency's trade regulation rule, titled Disclosure Requirements and Prohibitions Concerning Franchising and Business Opportunity Ventures. In essence, the FTC rules, which have been amended over time, are an attempt to remedy the problems of non-disclosure and misrepresentation that arise when people purchase franchises without first obtaining reliable information about them. The rules require franchisors and franchise brokers to furnish prospective franchisees with information about the franchisor, the franchisor's business, and the terms of the franchise agreement in one single document—the basic franchise disclosure document (go to www.entrepreneur.com/franchiseresources for an example).

Additional information must be furnished if any claims are made about actual or potential earnings. This is referred to as the *earnings claim document*. The franchisor must also give the franchisee a copy of the proposed franchise agreement. The disclosures must include important facts in terms of the franchisor-franchisee relationship.

The FTC rule does not require registration, but does require that you provide the potential franchisee with certain written disclosures at your first face-to-face meeting with them, and at least 14 calendar days before the franchisee signs any franchise agreement or other binding document or pays any consideration. Go to www.franchisebiblestudy.com for more details.

The FTC requires that the franchisor update the disclosure documents within 120 days of the close of the fiscal year. The franchisor must also prepare revisions within a reasonable time after the close of each quarter and attach them to or add them into the disclosure document to reflect any material change.

Prior to January 1, 1995, federal law preempted certain state laws where there was overlap in the laws. In other words, if both federal and state law covered an area, federal law controlled. Effective January 1, 1995, the FTC adopted a disclosure format known as the Uniform Franchise Offering Circular (UFOC) that could be used to comply with state registration laws. This eliminated some duplicate disclosure requirements under federal and state statutes. The requirements of the UFOC have been modified, and the document has been renamed the "franchise disclosure document" or "FDD" by an amended FTC rule that became effective on July 1, 2008. Go to www.franchisebiblestudy.com for a copy of the amended FTC rule.

> Due to the complexity of creating a disclosure document that meets all levels of legal requirements, it is not safe to attempt to complete this yourself. By following the sample franchise documents in the appendices, you can start to build the framework for your franchise documents that can be reviewed and completed by professionals. Doing this preliminary work will likely help you reduce your attorney fees.

A violation of the rules set forth by the FTC for failure to provide the required disclosure document or for misrepresentation will constitute an unfair or deceptive act or practice within the meaning of Section 5 of the Federal Trade Commission Act. It subjects the violator to civil penalty actions brought by the FTC of up to $10,000 in fines per violation per day. The courts have held that the FTC rule does not create a private right of action in wronged franchisees. In other words, the rule is enforced by the FTC and not by lawsuits filed by individuals. However, some franchisees have successfully sought enforcement of disclosure rules using state unfair practice acts.

Under federal law, as the franchisor, you must provide prospective franchisees with a disclosure document that conforms to the law, but you do not have to send a copy to the FTC or register the document with the FTC. In states requiring registration, such as California, you must complete an application for registration that contains, among other things, information regarding the background of the salespersons authorized to sell the franchise and you must pay state registration fees. Go to www.franchisebible study.com for more specifics on filing fees in franchise registration states.

State Law

Certain states have laws concerning franchising beyond the federal laws already mentioned. These states are referred to as *registration states*. Some new franchisors make the expensive mistake of registering in all of the registration states at the onset of their growth. You do not have to register in all of the registration states to become a franchisor. Consult with your franchise experts to develop a registration state strategy for your model.

REGISTRATION STATE REQUIREMENTS

Fourteen states have franchise registration or notice of filing acts: California, Hawaii, Illinois, Indiana, Maryland, Michigan, Minnesota, New York, North Dakota, Rhode Island, South Dakota, Virginia, Washington, and Wisconsin. If you want to sell franchises, these acts require that you file and gain approval of an application that contains information about who you are, submit a copy of your proposed contract, and prepare a proposed franchise disclosure document that is to be given to the franchisee a certain number of days before he or she purchases the franchise or pays any money for it.

Depending on your location, you may not have to concern yourself with state registrations right away. You are able to sell franchises in the 35 non-registration states with the appropriate franchise disclosure documents and no further state filings.

STATE RENEWAL AND TERMINATION LAWS

Laws regarding the termination and transfer of franchisees are commonly referred to as *franchise relationship laws*. Some of these termination and transfer laws are contained in state franchise investment or disclosure acts. Others are contained in a deceptive franchise act, pyramid scheme act, or retail franchising act and, in Wisconsin, the fair dealership law. For an abbreviated list of such laws, go to www.franchisebiblestudy.com.

In the absence of a state statute to the contrary, a fixed-term franchise that does not provide for general renewal will expire upon its expiration date. However, some of the state statutes require good cause for termination. The good-cause requirements in some of these franchise laws may mandate renewal of a fixed-term agreement, even one that clearly states that no renewal is allowed, thereby resulting in the perpetual renewal of the agreement unless the franchisor can prove that the franchisee did something that constituted good cause for termination of the agreement. Some states allow nonrenewal for specified reasons, including failure by the franchisee to agree to the standard terms of the renewal franchise. Other states have specific notice requirements regarding nonrenewal of a franchise agreement.

> These laws change from time to time and, therefore, it is imperative that any franchisor who does not intend to renew, or has a franchisee who is transferring his or her franchise, consult with an experienced legal counsel for the purpose of checking current law before issuing any communication to the franchisee.

Trademarks

If you have a product or service that is unique or in demand, you must capture this uniqueness through the use of a *trademark* (if it is a product) or *service mark* (if it is a service). The idea is to get the American public to associate your product with a particular trademark.

For many years, purchasers of a certain type of transparent tape would not go into the local stationery store and ask for transparent tape but would instead automatically ask for the trademarked "Scotch" tape. In looking around, you will see that all of the big companies utilize this concept. The producers of cola drinks do not want you to ask for just "a cola," thereby allowing the local dispenser of the product to make the choice for you. The Coca-Cola Company wants you to ask for a Coke, and the Pepsi-Cola Company wants you to ask for a Pepsi.

As a result, you will want to apply for a registered trademark or service mark on your product or service as soon as possible. You will most certainly want to do this before the first franchise agreement is negotiated and consummated. Keep in mind that the trademark or service mark must be used in intrastate and interstate commerce before the owner can apply to the U.S. Patent and Trademark Office (USPTO) in Washington, DC, to register it.

Before spending any money to advertise or promote a trademark or service mark, determine that no other entity has already secured the registered rights of that particular trademark or service mark. You can do so for less than $600 by contacting one of many trademark search firms. Thomson Compumark offers a variety of trademark searches including its "U.S. full availability search," which not only covers registered and pending marks in the USPTO, but also includes state, common law, and domain name coverage so you can determine if someone else may have a prior common-law right to use the mark, even though that person might not have registered it with the USPTO. It is possible that even with a registration certificate, some entity might have secured a common-law right in a particular area that is superior to your registration date. Be aware that some search firms will provide their services only to attorneys. Since your application for federal trademark or service mark registration will be reviewed and determined by a government attorney, it is advisable to retain a trademark attorney.

If you do not want to utilize such a search, you can make a preliminary search through the USPTO office pending and registered marks by going to www.uspto.gov and clicking on the Trademarks tab. This can be useful but it is not the most reliable type of search because it does not account for all potential sources of coverage. Then, after determining that you probably have a trademark that can be registered, your next step is to have it registered with the USPTO, and a trademark attorney can do this for you, usually for between $750 and $1,500.

The filing fees for trademark applications currently range from $275 to $375 depending on the type and form (electronic or paper) of the application. For more information on trademark registration, go to www.uspto.gov, which offers informational videos and documents on the trademark application process.

If the examiner determines that your trademark will not cause confusion with the trademarked goods of others that have registered pending registration with the USPTO, your application will be published in the Federal Register, allowing third parties to object if they disagree with the examiner. If there are no objections, you will receive a certificate of trademark registration approximately three to six months after your application has been published in the Federal Register. Your registered trademark will be in effect for ten years before it needs to be renewed.

Once you have received your certificate of trademark registration, you should let the world know you have it. Remember that once you have obtained a certificate of registration, you are eligible to seek enforcement of your trademark or service mark against infringers through litigation in federal district courts. In addition, you may register your trademark with state agencies, although this is not necessary if you have a federal registration. Registration laws vary from state to state, but most states require a nominal fee in the range of $20 to $150.

Financial Performance Representations

Some franchisors choose to include *financial performance representations* (FPRs) in their franchise disclosure documents. The FTC allows franchisors to include certain financials under Item 19 of the FDD as long as they numbers are real and can be validated by the franchisor. You can discuss the pros and cons of this option with your franchise attorney and franchise consultant.

Audited Financial Statement Requirements

The FTC requires that you insert the franchise entities audited financial statements as an exhibit to the franchise disclosure documents within three years of the starting your franchise company and there is a sequence to follow over the three-year period. Certain registration states will require audited financial statements to register in their states.

You will want to interview and choose an accounting firm that has an existing franchise practice and is familiar with franchise audit protocols. Work together with your franchise accountant to create your strategy and create a budget for the ongoing audit expenses.

Three Franchise Decision Lens Philosophy

Just because you can doesn't always mean that you should. This statement addresses the situation where you as a franchisor may have the legal right to take action against a franchisee but choose not to. You are building a community of franchise owners. Everything that you do on the corporate level will impact your franchisees in some way. The best method to manage your franchise organization's decisions is to apply the Three Franchise Decision Lens philosophy (see Figure 10-1).

Whenever you and your team have to make a decision or apply a new program or system that impacts the franchise community (which is just about anything and everything), make sure that you are looking directly through the middle lens. This gives you the ability to play out how the decision will impact your organization from the *legal, practical*, and *political* angles. *Legal* is mostly defined as any contractual relationships that you have with the franchise owners but may also take on other legal elements or considerations. *Political* encompasses the community issues and can be summed up as the way the franchise community feels about the franchise leadership. The *Practical* lens boils down to the actual logistics of carrying out something on a system-wide basis. The target in the middle represents the philosophy of considering all angles of each decision from these three perspectives for the best outcome.

Figure 10-1. Three Franchise Decision Lenses

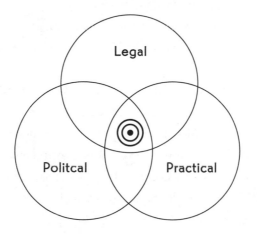

Consider the scenario of a potential change to your company's required equipment list. Legally you have the right to make the change based on your franchise agreement structure so no issues there. Practical implementation proves that it makes the most sense to phase this in by having all new owners start with the new equipment and giving the existing owners a ramp-up time-line so not to overwhelm your corporate resources. You decide to set up a franchise owner survey process to gather information to make the best political choice and find that the franchise owners are in favor but agree that a ramp-up period of 18 months makes the best sense.

> In the example you can see that a sudden decision based only on the legal lens could have resulted in hardships on the franchisee and backlash for your corporate team.

Disciplinary Actions

The purpose of the franchise legal documents is to create a strong, durable set of terms and conditions that you as the franchisor and the franchise owners mutually agree to in writing. A good contract seldom comes back out of the filing cabinet unless a franchisee is out of compliance or unhappy with the franchisor. The best way to avoid disputes is to make sure the franchise owners are happy and making money.

In the event that you must enforce a disciplinary action, consult with your franchise attorney to ensure the proper processes are utilized.

Transfer, Renewal, and Termination Clauses

You must select each of your franchisees carefully. Never sell a franchise to anyone you do not consider completely qualified for the job. The franchisee is also a manager of your business extension, so you should never choose as a franchisee someone you would not hire as a manager. A good selection of franchisees will diminish the chance of franchise failure, especially early transfers and terminations. Treat the franchisee like a member of your team and regard the franchising system as an extension of your marketing arm. It is your services or products that are being sold under your service mark or trademark. You would not hesitate to assist one of your company managers when in trouble or even to remove him or her if it were in the best interest of the company-owned office.

If you look upon the franchisee as a replacement for your company-owned office, your attitude will be positive when concentrating on assisting him or her. Your franchise agreement should allow for transfers, with your consent, which you should not withhold unreasonably. Examples of transfer and termination provisions are contained in the sample franchise agreement on www.franchisebiblestudy.com.

If a franchisee is dissatisfied, the best procedure is to allow him or her to transfer his operation or for you to buy out the franchisee. Lawsuits are costly and time-consuming, and you must report them in the disclosure document. Therefore, a lawsuit could be detrimental to the future sale of franchises, since potential franchisees will be made aware of the dissatisfied franchisees who are suing or have been terminated and these dissatisfied franchisees may give them negative information about you.

Franchise agreements are generally drafted by an attorney with provisions that are applicable in the state where the franchisor and the attorney are located. In many cases, the termination and transfer provisions may be contrary to the laws of other states where the same franchise agreement is being utilized. The cost of tailoring each clause to abide by changing laws in each state can be prohibitive. In addition, new state laws become effective from time to time after the initial franchise agreement has been drafted. Therefore, before any transfer is made, your attorney should check over the particular state law pertaining to transfers or terminations—even if there is a clause in your agreement stating that the laws of the state of the franchisor apply.

Operations Manual

As part of the operational function in a well-developed franchise system, you should prepare and provide an effective operations manual that documents the functions of the franchise business in a written, chronological, step-by-step format, so that the franchisee can easily follow them after completing the initial franchise training program.

You can have an all-purpose consultant prepare your operations manual, or, if you are an experienced business owner, you can do it yourself by following the sample operations manual outline in Figure 10-2 and merely listing, in chronological order—perhaps by talking into an audio recorder—the steps that complete the operations of your business. This account of basic business practices details the specific elements that made your business unique and successful. If you feel awkward doing this, you can have someone else record and subsequently type up what you have said regarding the basic functions of the business. The operations manual is generally used to establish the framework that you will use for training sessions.

If you feel you do not have the necessary dictation and writing skills to create a training manual, and if you do not have a family member or employee who can do so, hire a qualified person to write one. Individuals who specialize in writing manuals can be hired for fees as low as $2,000 to $5,000 for traditional manuals or upwards of $25,000 for more sophisticated online platforms. If any confidential information is to be contained in the manual, take steps to get a non-disclosure agreement from the person retained to write and/or type the manual and consider obtaining copyrights for the manual.

Each franchisor's operations manual is unique, because in a given industry each successful franchisor has a quality that distinguishes his or her business from those of the competitors. For example, a Wendy's operation featuring orders made up as they are given to the cashier differs from a McDonald's, where food is prepared in advance. Another illustration of this is Subway's method of making sandwiches at the direction of the customer, who deals with the individual preparer instead of ordering through a cashier.

Some franchisors have two operations manuals. One might deal with site selection, the initial opening of the store, bookkeeping, accounting, advertising, and grand-opening procedures. The second manual may address the duties of individual employees and, in the case of a restaurant, preparation of the food. A second manual could also cover such everyday duties as opening and closing procedures, accepting checks, making daily reports, hiring employees, preparing time sheets, receiving and transferring goods, preparing supply lists, and maintaining inventory procedures, security measures, and banking procedures.

Figure 10-2. Sample Operations Manual Outline (provided by Jumpstart Manuals)

THIS IS A SIMPLE OUTLINE. ADD SECTIONS THAT ARE SPECIFIC TO YOUR BUSINESS MODEL:

I. Introduction
  a)   Start-Up
  b)   Accounting
  c)   Employee Management
  d)   Safety and Security
  e)   Customer Service

f)   Marketing

g)   Sales

h)   Business Operations

II. Introduction Outline

a)   Manual Purpose and Organization

b)   Welcome to [Company]

c)   [Company] History

d)   Ethical Standards

e)   Legal and Regulatory

f)   Conclusion

III. Startup Outline

a)   General Guidelines

b)   Form the Business

c)   Obtain Business Licenses and Forms

d)   Business Accounting Records

e)   Insurance Requirements

f)   Hire Professional Support

g)   Initial Equipment Package

h)   Site Selection

i)   Computer Hardware and Software

j)   Additional Office Equipment

k)   [Company] Contact Information

l)   Training Requirements

m)   Grand Opening Procedures

n)   Conclusion

IV. Accounting Outline

a)   Financial Privacy and Confidentiality

b)   Roles and Responsibilities

c)   Benefits of Financial Management

d) Break-Even Point

e) Generally Accepted Accounting Practices (GAAP)

f) Benchmarks

g) Net Profit Margin

h) Hiring an Accountant

i) Accounting and Bookkeeping Methods

j) Chart of Accounts

k) Reports

l) Profit & Loss/Income Statement

m) Balance Sheet

n) Statement of Cash Flow

o) Payments to Franchise HQ

p) Retaining and Storing Records

q) Bookkeeping

r) General Accounting Procedure

s) Payment Transactions

t) Payroll

u) Taxess

v) Charitable Donations

w) Conclusion

V. Employee Management Outline

a) Introduction

b) Legal Issues Regarding Employees

c) Recommended Violence Prevention Policy

d) Best Practices: Recruiting and Selecting Employees

e) Example: Job Advertisement

f) Best Practices: Selecting Interview Candidates

g) Orientation / Training New Employees

h) Forms for Employee Management (Recommended Documents)

Safety & Security Outline

a) Introduction

b) Emergency Preparedness

c) Crisis Situations

d) Handling a Crisis

e) Job Site Safety

f) Employee Safety and Security Training

g) Electrical Safety

h) Safety Practices

i) Chemical and Materials Safety

j) Material Data Safety Sheet (MSDS)

k) Crime Prevention

Customer Service Outline

a) Introduction

b) Professionalism

c) Brand Standards and Personal Appearance

d) Phone Etiquette

e) On the Job Etiquette

f) Customer Preparation

g) Clean Up

h) Your [Company] Equipment

i) Handling Complaints

j) Handling Refund Requests

Marketing Outline

a) What is marketing?

b) [Company] Marketing Philosophy and Values

c) Marketing Materials

d) Guidelines for Using the [Company] Marks

e) How to Create a Marketing Budget

f) Advertising

g) Market to Your Community

h) Explanation of Social Media

i) Social Media Policy

j) Recommendations and Best Practices

k) Maintaining Social Media Networks

l) Social Media Resources

m) Training Employees to be Involved with Social Media

n) Social Media Marketing

o) Understand Your Competition

Sales Outline

a) Introduction

b) The [Company] Customer

c) Approach Family and Friends

d) First Spots to Hit

e) Business Sales Strategies and Processes

f) Cold Calling

g) [Company] Sales Presentations

Business Operations—Generic

a) Opening Checklist

b) Opening Checklist description

c) Post Rush-Shift Change Checklist

d) Post Rush-Shift Change description

e) Cleaning duties and checklists

f) Management checklists (mgr/asst., etc)

g) Duties explained

h) Specific Operational Procedures (varies depends on business)

Appendix

a) All forms used for the operations of the business

Conclusion

Legal considerations are part and parcel with the franchise business model due to the contractual relationships that you will have with multiple parties. The good news is, the FTC has established straightforward guidelines for franchisors to follow. A well-run franchise organization should have very little in the way of legal issues as long as the focus is to build a successful franchise community.

CHAPTER 11

Building a Strong Franchise Organization

Getting all of your documentation and materials completed alone does not make you a franchisor. Most would agree that you become an official franchisor once you have franchise owners who are open for business and successful. This chapter offers tips and strategies that you can apply to build a thriving franchise organization and community.

Company Infrastructure

As a would-be franchisor, you must realize that your current management, operating, and marketing techniques probably are insufficient in many ways for a successful franchise operation. For instance, a good computer sales employee is not necessarily a good computer franchise salesperson. A good field manager is not necessarily a good franchise manager, particularly when it comes to supervising multiple, independently operating franchisees. Company managers who have trained company employees informally, one on one, might not be qualified to adequately train a group of potential franchisees who have a significant amount of their savings at stake.

In addition, present advertising media suitable for selling a product or service at the retail level is not necessarily suitable for attracting qualified people with adequate capital interested in purchasing franchises. In short, your previous experience and knowledge of your business may not necessarily be the same experience and knowledge required to successfully operate a franchise business.

To be successful, a potential franchisor must have built his or her own business, no matter what size, on a sound foundation of well-trained personnel, good marketing techniques, and an adequate working capital structure. These foundation blocks are the same for a successful franchise operation as well, but as a franchisor you will need to view them from a different perspective and utilize different skills.

Franchise Glue

"Franchise glue" is a term that references all of the things, that you as a franchisor, offer the franchisees that "sticks them to you." In other words, all of the training, support, tools and technologies that help them grow their businesses. You want as much franchise glue as you can offer to make sure that your franchise owners have all the more reason to stick with you. Franchisors that have very little or weak glue find that franchisee fall away more easily. Commit to the following to avoid losing franchise owners:

- Avoid the "what have you done for me lately?" syndrome by always innovating and bringing new money-making ideas and concepts to your franchise owners.
- Start and maintain a company culture based on community that will carry through to the franchise owner's employees, customers and neighbors.
- Host regular continued education events and webinars to increase the over all success potential of the franchise community.
- Communicate regularly with your franchise owners just to check in to see how they are doing and to see if you can help with anything.

You will also want to continue to innovate and add more franchise glue as you grow to keep adding more value. You never want your franchisees to hesitate when they write their royalty check to question the value they are receiving.

Why Buy Your Franchise?

What makes your franchise special? Why would people want to invest their hard-earned money to buy your franchise over the others? These are questions to get you thinking about your franchise offering. You will want to offer your franchise owners training, support, and tools to make more money and spend less.

Franchise Bible Study: Complete the Franchise Hot Buttons exercise to establish the basis for your franchise offering message. Go to www.franchisebiblestudy.com and click the Franchise Your Business tab.

Buying Power, Approved Suppliers, and Other Revenue Sources

One common franchise glue benefit that will impress and help franchise owners is your ability to save them money for products, supplies, and services that they consume in the operation of their businesses. This is an example of collective *buying power* that a franchise organization can offer. This usually is in the form of discounted pricing that you can pass through to your franchisees from your *approved suppliers* that you will specify in your FDD and operations manual. You may be surprised to learn that your suppliers may be willing to offer "best pricing" once they are notified that you are franchising your business. Your suppliers will benefit by selling more as your franchise network grows, so they should be willing to work with you to keep your relationship. If they are not, it is a good time to shop suppliers and seek the ones that see the value in your future plans.

You may find *other revenue sources* that become available to you with these new vendor relationships. They may come as bonuses or rebates. You may even have a markup on certain items. Most franchise owners don't mind if you make money on these items as long as it is still a good deal for them.

> A good rule of thumb is to make sure that the pricing you offer the franchisees is lower than what they could get on their own.

Facility Evaluation and Selecting Your Central Office

A common challenge for new franchise organizations is their first impression to prospective franchise owners when they are just starting out. Most "early adopters" understand that a new franchisor is in their growth stage and may not have a big impressive headquarter. Once you are ready to start planning your first franchise "discovery day" events, you will want to evaluate your current facilities. Your prospective franchise owners are going to invest their hard-earned money to buy your franchise and they have to feel confident when they meet with you and your team.

SELECTING YOUR CENTRAL OFFICE

In many cases, one of the first things new franchisors do is commit themselves and their new franchise company to a costly new office showplace. This can be fatal. You must do the same thing for yourself as you do for the franchisee: establish a highly capable, efficient organization at the lowest cost possible. You should have a pilot unit of the operation you are intending to franchise. Often, you can initially work from this location for company tours and training and use offsite facilities for meetings and presentations.

FRANCHISE AND BUSINESS INCUBATORS AND ACCELERATOR FACILITIES

Cooperative workspaces such as executive offices and incubator or accelerator facilities are also a good option for emerging brands. These buildings will usually offer office space, meeting rooms, and other services such as phone answering and front desk reception and allow your company to grow to a larger space as you onboard more franchisees and staff.

> Budget, budget, budget! Your success or failure can be determined in many instances by how well you plan your initial operation. Thus, plan your franchise operation in the same careful way as you have planned your business and the future business operations of your franchisees.

Growth and Staffing Plan

You will want to create a business growth and staffing plan that includes a budget. One common mistake that new franchisors make is adding too much, too fast when it comes to overhead. This includes labor dollars in the

> Avoid nepotism at all costs when you build your franchise team. Choose your team members carefully based on the most qualified prospects. Avoid hiring family members because they need a job or they were around when you started out. Having to fire your sister makes for an awkward Thanksgiving dinner.

form of salaries for executives and support staff. You may need to work on a skeleton crew budget until you have enough revenue from franchise fees, royalties, and other franchise income to justify the added cost of more staff. You may have to be CEO and chief bottle washer for a while.

WELL-TRAINED PERSONNEL

Your success really lies in your ability to recognize the business insight necessary to operate a smooth-running, successful franchise. To help you do this, carefully review your current management, marketing, training, advertising, and sales personnel to determine whether you should provide franchise management training, engage specialized consultation for present personnel, and/or hire new personnel. The capabilities of current personnel should be carefully reviewed and, where they are found lacking in franchise experience, they should be properly trained in franchise operating and marketing techniques.

Staffing a well-run franchise operation with knowledgeable, competent personnel can be achieved at a reasonable expense in one of four ways:

- Educating current personnel
- Hiring experienced franchise personnel
- Subcontracting for franchise functions
- Retaining an all-purpose franchise consultant

Educating Current Personnel

In many cases, current employees may be a great fit for the franchise team that you are going to build. You will likely be able to identify key staff members that can fill franchise roles as you grow. This can be an exciting new opportunity for certain team members. Consider the following tips:

- Be sure that you have a real need for the positions. Do not create positions for people just to accommodate them if it is not a benefit for the company.
- Create a job description for each position and interview individuals for each.
- Be sure that the candidates are enthusiastic and qualified for the respective positions.
- Don't be surprised if you experience jealousy and lack of participation or interest from your staff members who are not a part of your new franchise business.

Hiring Experienced Franchise Personnel

The second method of ensuring adequate personnel familiar with current franchising methods is to hire experienced personnel who have worked for other franchisors. You should thoroughly review not only each applicant's franchise expertise but also his or her character and knowledge of current franchising laws. An applicant's basic knowledge of franchising could be based on methods now prohibited by franchise laws—methods such as providing actual or projected revenue and sales figures to potential franchisees and/or negotiating material terms of a franchise agreement without proper government approval. Thus, ensure that employee applicants are familiar with not only current franchise marketing techniques, but also the numerous legal restrictions that franchises may face.

Hiring additional experienced franchise personnel can be costly and it may not be necessary if you are a smaller franchisor. In many cases, the smaller franchisor will handle all the administrative, management, and marketing functions of his or her new franchise operation, at least initially. Therefore, if your franchise plan is to start with a small or medium-sized franchise system (maybe limited to one or two states), you may prefer educating current personnel about franchising rather than hiring high-priced new personnel with prior franchise experience.

Subcontracting for Franchise Functions

The third and highly recommended way of educating yourself and your staff on the business aspects of franchising is to subcontract the job to individual franchise specialists in the fields of law, training, advertising, public relations, and marketing. These consultants will evaluate your needs and, instead of providing a complete package, will give you only what you actually need.

The one outside professional that is always necessary is an experienced franchise attorney who understands not only franchise law but the everyday business aspects of franchising. Talk to the attorney's past franchise clients about his or her legal expertise and hands-on knowledge of franchising.

When selecting an advertising agency, make sure it is one that specializes in franchising as well as general business. The same holds true with financing and marketing specialists. Carefully check each specialist's references.

Retaining an All-Purpose Franchise Consultant

This can be a very efficient solution, especially in the case of a small company with very little existing infrastructure. The consultant will usually be able to offer structure and support as well as advice and direction to enable you to build your company. Be sure to interview the consultants to make sure that they are a good fit for your company. Make sure they are franchise experts and have a track record of successful franchise clientele.

In addition, the all-purpose consultant may provide services for the creation of your operations manuals, video training platforms, and feasibility market and business plan assistance.

Conclusion

This chapter covered tips and strategies that you can apply to your franchise organization. How you build your franchise infrastructure will determine how fast you can grow, how fast your franchisees can grow, and how profitable your overall company becomes. Take the time to build your strong franchise organization right the first time.

Strategize to Thrive!

"To flourish or develop successfully" is a Webster's definition of the word *thrive*. This chapter contains "the secret sauce" that can set you apart from the competitors in your category. You can apply the tips here to define your company strategy and culture and establish your company as the obvious choice.

You Can't Just "Try" Franchising

In order to get in the right mindset to truly build a thriving franchise company, you must first commit to starting and running a "whole new business." This may seem like a given, but some have franchised without this simple commitment and ultimately failed. Sometimes one's successful business can inadvertently end up as a franchise. This usually occurs when the people (employees, friends, family, and customers) around a business owner convince them that they should franchise and if they do they will be wildly successful.

Having a great business is certainly the prerequisite for franchising, but not the only one. You must be ready, willing, and able to become a franchisor. As it is sometimes said, "you don't *try* franchising"—you either become a franchisor or you don't.

Choosing the Best Franchise Owners

The temptation to sell a franchise to the wrong person can be very strong and always seems to come at the worst time, like when things are tight and the added cash flow would be a huge help. Erv Keup often said, "You will want to buy back your first ten franchises at twice the price just to see them go." When asked why, he revealed that new franchisors get so excited that they sell to anyone that will buy, not necessarily the best and most qualified prospects.

AWARDING VS. SELLING

You will often hear the terms "franchise sales" or "selling franchises" as you enter the franchise world. This is a common reference but is not an entirely accurate definition. The best term is *award* a franchise. This is due to the process that franchisors implement during their recruiting and discovery processes. Even though the franchisee is "buying" a franchise, the franchisor is ultimately choosing them based on a variety of qualifications (hopefully not just financial).

EARLY ADOPTERS

Early adopters are individuals that tend to "buy in" early. These are the folks who sleep in front of the Apple Store for three days to be the first to own the new iPhone. They have a sense of adventure when it comes to trying new things. While others may want to see a more proven track record, early adopters will be your first franchise owners. They thrive on ground floor opportunities and love the challenge and rewards of growing with a new concept.

Be sure to embrace these daring souls and reward them with opportunities as they grow with you. Also make sure that they get the "good stuff," even though your company is a startup. You don't want the "first child syndrome" to happen and hear them say "I didn't get the cool stuff like the new franchisees get now."

EARLY ENTHUSIASTS DON'T ALWAYS WORK OUT

Early enthusiasts are different from early adopters. An adopter is willing to "adopt" or take on something in its entirety, much like adopting a child is a total commitment. An early enthusiast is anyone who is excited about your "exploding national company" and wants to ride the coattails for all the wrong reasons.

It is nice to have enthusiastic people around, but they can turn out to be disasters if they become franchise owners. The best rule is to put every franchise lead through the same thorough discovery process regardless of who they are or where they came from.

Happy Franchise Owners Make More Money

This is a statement that sums up the essence of a healthy franchise system. The word *happy* implies the highest level of satisfaction, which is the place where people tend to perform their best.

The franchisors that constantly strive for "happy franchisees" focus on the true elements that will help them grow their businesses, which in turn, grows their business too.

BUILD YOUR ORGANIZATION WITH A SERVANT ATTITUDE

The best way to ensure that you have happy franchise owners is to adopt a *servant attitude* much like the hospitality industry. We have seen service-based business models give their customers an awesome servant level of service only to treat their franchisees poorly. Franchising is a one-of-a-kind industry, and that attitude does not work.

UPSIDE-DOWN PYRAMID PHILOSOPHY

This is a strategy to illustrate the total reversal of the common corporate business model that works best for franchise organizations (see Figure 12-1). A typical corporate structure places the boss (CEO or president) at the top of the pyramid "managing" the people in the organization.

Franchising works best when you turn the pyramid upside-down and carry the weight of the franchise community squarely on the shoulders of the franchise training and support team. With this model the leader (CEO or president) is at the bottom serving and inspiring up to the training and support team and the franchise community, employees, and customers (win, win, win, and win).

Figure 12-1. Upside-down pyramid structure for franchising

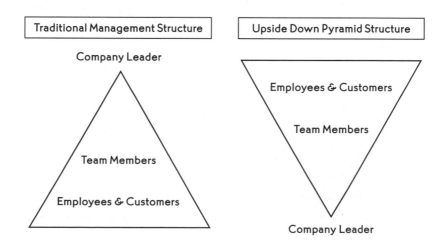

Inspiration vs. Motivation

We learned this lesson from one of Rick's franchise owners when he was the leader of his franchise company. The company was growing fast, and Rick was soul searching to figure out how to be a better leader. Rick told him that he needed to become a motivational leader. The franchise owner quickly corrected him and said, "if I was walking the plank with a sword poking me in the back that would motivate me, but not in a good way." He continued to tell Rick that what he truly wanted as a franchise owner was to be "inspired," not "motivated"—which was a very valuable lesson.

Choosing Franchise Experts

Throughout this book, you are advised to consult a competent attorney who preferably specializes in franchise law to assist you in the franchising arena. The attorney's assistance can range from putting together the required disclosure documents to researching federal and state franchise laws.

Because franchise attorneys have gone through the franchise process before, they can be of particular help to new franchisors who are not familiar with the training, marketing, administrative, and sales functions that are unique to a franchising operation.

Another important area where franchise attorneys can be of assistance is in the marketing of your potential franchise. For many potential franchisees, the disclosure document is the first point-of-sale piece they see. Your disclosure document introduces you, presents your background and those of your predecessors, and outlines all the services, products, and obligations. Having an experienced, franchise-oriented attorney help you prepare your disclosure document effectively and accurately could prove very valuable, both in terms of marketing and in terms of complying with federal and state franchise laws.

A disclosure document must have provisions that are practical, time-proven, business-oriented, workable, and, above all, fair. Because most executives of a prospective franchisor entity, whether large or small, have no prior experience in operating a franchise business and not much, if any, know-how in selling franchises, training franchisees, or opening and servicing franchises, they are of little help to the franchise attorney from a business standpoint. As a result, the situation arises in which the attorney is required to know much more about franchising than his or her client does, in addition to knowing the legal requirements. Therefore, you should find out whether your franchise attorney is more than a legal technician whose only function is to file a legally acceptable document to get you a permit from the state authority to sell franchises.

When you and your experienced, market-oriented attorney begin work on the disclosure document and franchise agreement, you should have already made certain decisions, including the franchise fee to be charged, the type of training to be given to the franchisees, the continuing royalty and service fees to be charged, and the duties and obligations of both the franchisor and the franchisee. All such business decisions should be made based on time-proven, practical policies that are designed to assist, and not detract from, the overall success of the franchise system.

If you fail to properly prepare yourself for operating a franchise system, including selecting either a business-minded, franchise-oriented attorney or an experienced, business-oriented franchise consultant, you may be launching your new franchise the same way as you started the business you intend to franchise—with absolutely no practical knowledge of how to operate it.

Chances are the attorney you have used in the past will be in the same boat when it comes to franchising the business. You both may have started out as novices in the business startup world, but through trial and error and working together, you have gained business know-how and developed proven procedures for business success. Now that you have reached the point of expanding your business through franchising, that attorney may not be the one you want to rely on for determining such franchise factors as suitable franchise fees and royalties, setting up and operating a franchise, and the franchise agreement. Trial-and-error methods of operating a franchise company seldom succeed because such companies are operating with other people's money and they exist for a limited time.

If you have knowledge and experience in opening a franchise or you have guidance from a consultant or a new employee who has actual experience in running a successful franchise company, you or your employee or consultant can tell the attorney what procedural rules are necessary for a workable franchise agreement.

LEGAL FEES: WHAT TO EXPECT

Attorney fees can vary depending on economic conditions, location, and attorney overhead expenses and experience. However, an experienced attorney in most geographical markets who runs a cost-efficient operation can usually make a fair return on a flat fee rate between $20,000 to $50,000 (depending on the complexity of the business, knowledge of the franchisor, and how much research and information the franchisor has gathered) for preparing and filing a marketable, workable, and well-coordinated disclosure document in the initial state of the franchise.

Attorneys should be able to complete their work within 30 to 90 days, barring any unforeseen circumstances. Legal fees for each additional state (since the disclosure document will have to be amended in certain states) will vary, but should be much less than the fee for the initial state because much of the information for the second document will have already been compiled. Filing fees in registration states range from $250 to $750. You should obtain from the attorney a complete fee quotation for the initial state and for additional states, along with his or her scheduled date of completion.

Aside from legal costs, remember the cost of a certified audit, which is an initial necessity in certain states and an ultimate necessity in others. Generally, a good

> Be very cautious of attorneys who seek hourly fee arrangements with no cap on the total amount. Fees can escalate quickly. Also be cautious of high hourly rates. Higher rates do not necessarily equal better quality. Many attorneys will be able to provide a total estimated fee up front so that you can incorporate the cost into your start-up budget.

franchise attorney will have a client start a new corporation or LLC for the purpose of franchising; the audited financials of the new entity can be nominal—from an estimated $1,000 to $2,000, depending again upon the accountant's location, experience, and his or her cost effectiveness.

> Insist upon references from the attorney, and call each reference. Ask each client's opinion of the attorney's legal abilities and his or her ability to draft a disclosure document and franchise agreement that are fair, marketable, and marketing-oriented— all of which are necessary elements of a successful franchise operation.

As with any professional consultant, you cannot necessarily judge a good franchise attorney by their legal fees; you can, however, judge franchise attorneys by what their franchise clients say about them, not only in terms of complying with certain laws and regulations but also in terms of familiarity with the time-proven and correct methods of operating a franchise in a particular industry.

Registration State Strategy

As covered earlier in this book, there is a combination of non-registration and registration states in the United States. This section is less about the legal aspect and more about how you can plan to thrive by adopting a registration state strategy. Because the registration states require additional costs and effort, you will want to consider the following:

- Post a list of the non-registration and registration states for your development team to access anytime.
- Obtain a fee estimate from your franchise attorney for all registration states including the filing fees and legal fees so you can budget.
- Don't register in all of the states at once because it will be very expensive and the registrations are only good for one year and then have to be renewed.
- Choose to register in the states that make the most sense for your

business model. For instance, an ice cream franchise may choose warmer climates first.

- Create a game plan to make the most of your registration investment. Try to focus on the available markets within the respective states as soon as you are approved.

- Target your sales efforts. You only have to register in the registration states when you intend to sell new franchises within that year, so it will save money if you move from one market to the next instead of jumping around the map.

> A simple strategy as you grow is to start close to home. Your first few franchise launches will need extra attention, training, and support from you and your team (which may be just you in the beginning). You will also want to carefully track these first franchises to learn the intricacies of the onboarding and opening process. This is easier when you are close by. Trying to open your first franchise across the country is a bad idea for obvious reasons.

Conclusion

This chapter reveals some insider secrets to thrive as a franchisor. Apply these strategies to go above and beyond the call of duty and build your franchise community for success. Franchise success boils down to many little as well as big elements, best practices, and strategies.

CHAPTER 13

Building Your Franchise Community

Remember the upside-down pyramid from Chapter 12? Building your franchise community to thrive as a strong network will be the foundation that can support a huge company. Use the tips and ideas in this section to build your successful franchise community.

Creating Your Franchise Support Systems and Team

Your franchise support team will be the core of your community. Like a coaching staff that directs the team from the sidelines, your corporate office should be there to guide your franchisees so they can focus on playing their positions. Apply the following to build your support team:

- Be sure that your support team is on the same page and that they understand and believe in the company objectives and philosophy.
- Adopt a "show me" attitude based on leading by example. Be sure your support team can "play all of the positions" that your franchise owners play.
- Use communication software such as an intranet or *contact relationship management* (CRM) platform
- Make sure that all support staff make complete notes *every* time they communicate with franchise owners.

USING TECHNOLOGY FOR SUPPORT AND TRAINING

Support and training have become much more robust in today's world. Not too many years ago, franchisors had to assemble their franchise owners in-person for training sessions and delivered support by phone or mail.

It was common to hold back new developments until the annual convention, which was the only time everyone was together. Now franchisors can utilize web meetings and video conferencing to train and support franchisees whenever the need arises. This dynamic technology allows today's franchisors to disseminate new information more quickly and efficiently so owners can apply in the field immediately.

THE IDEAL FRANCHISE CANDIDATE MATRIX

Your ideal franchise candidate matrix will enable you to add the best franchisee team players. You can establish this matrix in a number of ways depending on your business model and the size of your company. Once you have franchise owners who have been operating for a while, you can establish a baseline for the success factors to look for in future franchisees. Also keep in mind that the ideal franchisee is not you. You must have a realistic idea of what the ideal owner looks like.

Generally, franchisees who continually want to change systems or have suggestions for change based purely on theory do not make the best franchisees. The ideal franchisee should have advisory input abilities but not the stubbornness to insist upon changing the franchise system, at least until the franchisee's theories are tested or the franchisee can show, based on experience, that such theories work.

In any potential franchisee, look for the same qualities that made you successful in operating your retail business. There are business consultants who research and identify the profile of ideal franchisees for various industries and companies. It might be a good idea to retain such a consultant if his or her clients have provided good references. In many ways, good common sense and an objective view of what is necessary, as determined by your past experience or your operational personnel, might be the ticket to determining the best profile for the ideal franchisee.

ASSISTING FRANCHISEES AS THEY NAVIGATE THE DISCOVERY AND LAUNCHING PROCESS

Your franchise development department (which again, may be you) has an important job to do. Choosing the best franchise candidates out of all of the inquiring shoppers is a challenge in today's world. You will want to set up a step-by-step discovery process that will guide prospective owners. You will want to have a consultative approach to educate them about your franchise opportunity without pressuring or "selling" them.

The best outcome for all parties is a great match between the franchisor and the franchise owners. Due to this fact, it is well worth the time investment to help your prospects navigate your process. This will result in more solid owners that have a higher probability of succeeding.

ASSISTING WITH SITE SELECTION

If your franchise involves a restaurant or other business in which location is a key factor in franchise sales, you will want to have someone assist your franchisees in selecting sites. Most franchisors require their franchisees to conduct preliminary research on potential sites. In most cases, real estate brokers or shopping-center managers can provide the demographics and other commercial information pertaining to each potential site.

The primary reason for making your franchisees responsible for site selection is not only to make the franchisee thoroughly familiar with the pros and cons of each potential site location, but also to help alleviate any liability you may face if you are the sole selector of the site and the franchisee subsequently fails. Many franchisees who fail will blame the choice of site location as the primary reason for their failure, even though the failure may be entirely the franchisee's own fault. Therefore, most franchisors require the franchisees to make their own site selection, with the franchisor acting as the final approving authority.

To ensure that the franchisee has picked an appropriate site, however, you should have a qualified broker or other expert evaluate the suitability of the chosen site. This person should be qualified in real estate matters and have some experience in franchising and in the particular business being franchised. In some cases, a new franchisor may act as the site selection appraiser assisting the franchisee; however, most franchisors retain real estate consultants rather than hire full-time personnel, at least in the initial stages. These agents normally are compensated by brokers' fees from the landlord. Again, carefully check out references and accomplishments of the brokers or individuals you hire to help your prospective franchisee find a franchise location.

COSTS OF PROVIDING SITE SELECTION ASSISTANCE

If you and/or the franchisee are knowledgeable regarding the elements necessary for a good site for the business and conduct the site selection yourselves, costs will be minimal. If contacts are made with local real estate brokers who are familiar with your franchisees' needs and territories, costs will also be minimal. Hiring a professional, full-time site selector could be expensive, depending upon your location. In most cases, an employee hired as a site selector will hold other positions in a franchise company, including marketing or training responsibilities. Again, try to keep your costs at a minimum without sacrificing the effectiveness of your organization.

Avoid the "Franchise Doldrums"

The *franchise doldrums* typically occur between 11 and 24 units. This is the stage where a franchisor runs out of what we call the "inner circle" buyers. These are the early enthusiasts and early adopters that tend to jump on board in the beginning of a franchisor's launch. At this point they often realize that they are stuck because they don't have any more leads and have to figure out how to compete with all the other franchisors on a national level. The best antidote for the franchise doldrums is an aggressive, fully comprehensive franchise marketing campaign that includes all of the elements that we discussed in the marketing chapter.

Becoming a Great Event Coordinator

Creating and hosting great franchise events can become the source of inspiration and growth for your overall franchise community. Apply the following strategies as you develop your company events:

- Be organized. Get a good written plan in place well in advance of every event. This reduces stress and ensures a smoother event day.
- Consider hiring an event coordinator for "pre-event" and/or "day of" coordination if you don't have an in-house coordinator on your staff.
- Commit to a professional production. Regardless of the size of the event, make sure that the audience or attendees experience a professional and polished production. Think of presentations and events that impressed you in the past. You will be judged on your professionalism.

Creating and Hosting Discovery/Decision Day Events

Even though you may be starting small, you will want to create your standard discovery/decision day event. This is a professional step for your franchise company. Remember the *Field of Dreams* movie quote? "If you build it, they will come." It's a more eloquent statement than, "fake it till you make it," but the message is similar. You will build good habits that will pay off in the future by practicing them while you are starting out.

Complete the discovery day exercise as you prepare for your first discovery day event by going to the Franchise My Business tab at www.franchisebiblestudy.com.

Forming and Managing Your Owner's Advisory Committee

One common complaint that franchisors get from the initial franchisees is in the area of early day support and resources, or lack thereof. One of the strategies you will want to employ is the formation and management of a properly run franchise owner's advisory committee. This is an advisory only (not voting or directing) committee of chosen or elected franchise owners that serve for a period of time or "term" that you specify.

This committee can help bring new ideas and topics of concern to the corporate team and also communicate with, and mentor newer franchisees.

Complete the franchise owner's advisory committee exercise as you prepare for your first owner's advisory committee event by going to the Franchise My Business tab of www.franchisebiblestudy.com.

MEETINGS AND CONVENTIONS

As mentioned earlier, a franchise organization is unique among most business structures. You have a large team spread out all over the country instead of being on the same playing field together.

Due to this reality, the annual convention and other company-wide meetings are usually highly anticipated by all. This is a fun and energizing time for both the franchise community and your franchise support team.

Focus on vision building as well as no-nonsense business-building tools anytime you gather your "party."

Offering Franchise Rewards and Incentive Programs

Franchisors should initiate a franchise rewards and incentive program from the very beginning (remember, "If you build it, they will come"). Start with standard annual goal-related objectives or contests, such as highest revenue, fastest growth, and highest customer satisfaction. Create awards that they can display in their office. This is a good method for sparking some fun and healthy competition. You can also create financial incentives for certain achievement levels as well. As your company grows, you may have more extravagant incentives, such as trips or big-ticket items.

Military Veteran Resources

U.S. military veterans are coming out of the military in large numbers. Many of these American heroes are returning to very little opportunity. They are also leaving a very structured environment and their military family and support system. Your franchise organization has the opportunity to embrace veterans and invite them into your franchise family as franchise owners. Many vets are seeking business ownership these days as opposed to seeking a job. Veterans are usually very good franchise owners since they are accustomed to following systems.

Conclusion

Building your franchise community is a mission-critical step in the long-term success of your franchise story. It is a subject that you don't hear much about or see in many franchise books or websites. This is probably due to the fact that it is less tangible than other, more obvious subjects. Your franchise *community* is the feeling of belonging and purpose that the owners feel and believe in, which in turn inspires them to press on and thrive.

CHAPTER 14

Franchise Marketing

This chapter aims to help you as a franchisor make the most of your franchise marketing and recruiting efforts. You may have the best franchise business model in the world, but you can't grow if no one knows about you.

Finding qualified franchise buyers can be the most challenging element of your franchise endeavors. Technology has had a huge impact on the way people research and buy franchises. You can use the concepts in this chapter to implement a comprehensive, multi-faceted marketing program to set you apart from your competitors and enjoy consistent growth.

Decades of Traditional Marketing

In the late 1960s and early '70s, as franchising began to gain momentum in the U.S. market and a variety of companies became available, franchisors had to determine the most cost-effective way to market their franchises to consistently bring in new franchise buyers. Before high technology was the status quo, franchisors found traditional marketing to be most effective. Traditional marketing included direct mail, print advertisements, trade shows, and eventually TV and radio.

Game Changer: the Internet and Beyond

Before the internet, franchisors used traditional marketing methods to attract prospective franchise buyers to in-person meeting events. These events consisted of tradeshows and expos, seminars and presentations, discovery days, and individual meetings. These personal experiences increased the trust level for the franchisors as well as the prospective franchisees. These events were naturally expensive and time-consuming, so franchisors welcomed the high-tech and cheaper alternative that the internet offered.

When the internet came along, there was a mass exodus from the live events to "virtual events" such as online tradeshows, advertising portals, and franchise clearing houses. These options promised low-cost, 24-hour convenience, stay-at-home benefits, and much more. To most franchisors this made good sense, but then they experienced a loss of the personal experience. It was like asking someone to marry you over the phone or by email. Buying a business is one of the biggest decisions a person will make in life. This "technology backlash" caused many to return to the basics.

A Little U.S. Franchise History

It is surprising to most people that McDonald's was not the first franchise in American history. The first was the Singer Corporation selling sewing machines in the 1800s. By the time McDonalds came around, many businesses had already expanded through franchising, including Arthur Murray, Baskin Robbins, and Orange Julius. In the 1950s, a milkshake machine salesman named Ray Croc connected with the McDonalds brothers, who owned a small hamburger stand. He brought the McDonald's franchise to the American population, and today it's one of the strongest and most well-known franchises in the world.

Back to Basics: Regaining the Discovery Process

Franchisors realized that the online experience was good for some things, such as convenience and the ability to efficiently communicate and exchange information. On the downside, it reduced the amount of personal interaction and commitment between the franchisor and prospective franchisees. The franchisors, despite the reduction in the marketing budget, realized they needed to invest time and money to regain a quality franchise discovery process. They began revisiting some of the traditional marketing methods in combination with the high-tech options available to them. The most successful franchisors have found a balance by using technology to expedite their communication, combined with an in-person experience with their franchisee prospects. Franchisors with a strong website and email follow-up or newsletters, along with an array of personal discovery experiences that not only offer the franchise buyer convenience but also demand personal commitment, are often in a better position to successfully enter into a franchisor-franchisee relationship.

As franchisors decided to revitalize some of their preexisting marketing efforts by revisiting the basics of traditional marketing, they brought with them the experiences, successes, and challenges of the technology that had changed marketing so drastically in the last decade. As an example, they may implement a direct-mail campaign that is reinforced by a direct-email campaign, with links in the email to a sweepstakes page or to a Request Information page on their website. They may use social media sites like Facebook, Twitter, and LinkedIn to announce their presence at a franchise exposition and offer free passes for those who register on their website. Another example would be placing traditional print advertising in franchise industry magazines in combination with an e-newsletter announcing their attendance with an electronic form for preregistration. All of these are examples of the combination of traditional marketing along with the more high-tech marketing that has become available in recent years.

Leveling the Playing Field

A beneficial outcome of the introduction of technology to the franchise industry is the reality that the playing field has been leveled for all franchisors in the U.S. and around the world. Not too long ago, franchisors had to have a large marketing budget to enable them to compete in a national or international marketplace. This is one reason why you think of major brands like McDonald's and Subway and other household names when you think about franchising. With the onset of technology, we have seen the smaller franchise brands compete by utilizing creative technology campaigns that have enabled them to gain market share without having huge marketing budgets. In today's market the most creative and innovative franchisors are able to gain the lion's share of the franchise prospects by utilizing the internet, websites, and social media to give them the edge over their competition.

Redefining the Basics of Marketing: The Five Pillars of Marketing

As we said in Chapter 1, if you think of marketing as a building, the pillars that give marketing structure are advertising, direct mail, sales, promotions, and public relations. Those categories make up the overall umbrella of the term we know as *marketing*. Most companies don't clearly define these categories and assign resources to each to maximize their overall marketing efforts. The most successful franchisors have been able to break down the five pillars of marketing, assign the appropriate resources, track their return on investment, and continue to fine-tune and adapt as the results vary. There are many specialists and consultants who can assist you in developing an overall marketing and execution plan. See Chapter 1 for more on the five pillars of marketing. Here we will recap the most important aspects of these pillars.

ADVERTISING

Advertising is made up of several sub-categories. You may think of advertising as print media only. The truth is, advertising encompasses any media that allows you to purchase space to promote your marketing message. This includes print advertising such as magazines, newspapers, and other printed formats, TV advertisements, radio advertisements, billboards, and now, with the onset of technology, it includes internet advertisements, websites, and more. The franchisors who create innovative advertising campaigns across all platforms realize the best return on investment (ROI).

DIRECT MAIL

Most of us think of direct mail as postcards that we receive in our mailbox. This is still an effective option depending on the strength of the message and the offer. With the onset of technology, other direct mail options are e-newsletters, drip email campaigns (a series of email messages sent to a prospect over a short period of time), and other opt-in alternatives that send information via the internet.

SALES

An effective sales process is a must for every franchise system. It's imperative for every franchisor to have a systematic, step-by-step discovery process for their prospective franchise buyers to follow. This process should be simple to understand, since the prospective franchisee needs to have the information presented to them in such a way that they can absorb it, weigh the pros and cons, and eventually make an educated decision. Methods of sales in the franchise world break down into the following sub-categories:

- Person-to-person sales that you might experience at a tradeshow, discovery day, or other discovery experience that the franchisor participates in.
- Phone sales that take place on either an outgoing or incoming basis. It's important as a franchisor to have a designated in-house franchise sales expert who is trained in the entire franchise process so this person can present the opportunity to the prospective franchisee effectively, answer questions, and handle objections.
- Outgoing phone sales, sometimes called *telemarketing*, can also be effective. It is far more challenging today to launch an effective telemarketing campaign due to caller ID, do-not-call lists, and voicemail. The important element of outgoing phone sales is to ensure that you are offering the franchise buyer information that is important to them and that provides them with an incentive to continue the discovery process with you.
- Technology has expanded the sales process. Email, texting, web presentations, and calendar syncing are as much a part of the franchise sales process as any traditional sales tool.

> Learn and apply the basics of negotiating. Know your bottom line before you enter the room and always have *all* of the decision-makers present. Never allow yourself or your team to get "too big for your britches" syndrome, which means you stay grounded. Some franchisors start to neglect or mistreat their franchisees as they gain success, which in turn can destroy their company.

You will find that the best candidates will follow your discovery steps, will seldom miss appointments, and will quickly get back to you when you leave messages. This is a good indicator of their ability to follow a system and of their enthusiasm and interest in your franchise concept. It also gives you an idea of their potential to be a successful business owner. One powerful tool is to utilize franchise-specific contact relationship management (CRM) software to keep track of your franchise prospects and their progress as they move through your sales pipeline.

PROMOTIONS

Traditionally promotions have been used to spark awareness and excitement in a marketing message. You have seen promotions like midnight madness sales, 24-hour sales, sweepstakes, giveaways, special events, customer appreciation dinners—or any kind of special, out-of-the-ordinary promotion that is utilized by various companies to attract new buyers or existing buyers back again. Successful franchisors use a combination of traditional promotions and promotions that utilize new technologies. For instance, they may hold a sweepstakes advertised in traditional media such as print, billboards, radio, and TV while also running the promotion on Facebook, Twitter, and other social media outlets. The internet options have given franchisors a low-investment way to reach masses of prospective buyers, allowing the smaller brand franchises to compete favorably with the bigger brands.

PUBLIC RELATIONS

Public relations may be the most underused pillar of marketing. Traditionally, public relations campaigns would consist of press releases, press kits, sponsorships, and other goodwill events and campaigns that would usually bring brand awareness through publicity. In the internet age, we have found that public relations is still a very viable and important pillar that needs attention. However, the delivery has changed considerably, and in some ways technology has made it far easier to launch a successful PR campaign.

An example of this may be a press release that in years past would have to be printed, put into a press kit, and mailed to 100 or 200 news and other media outlets hoping that the individuals at those outlets would find it interesting enough to write it into an article or a category of one of their existing articles or stories. It was difficult to measure success with this technique. Today, successful franchisors enjoy the ability to release their newsworthy articles via blogs and on industry and business startup blog platforms. In most cases this is free, and the more creative and informational the articles are, the more traffic they will draw. This method is also measureable since the analytics can be evaluated at the franchisor level and fine-tuned.

As you can see, the five pillars of marketing are alive and well, and probably always will be. These pillars have existed since people began to sell products and services to each other, although the delivery of the marketing message has changed.

Internet/Technology: The Sixth Pillar

As covered in Chapter 1, the internet has become a standalone sixth pillar of marketing. This section reveals the "best practices" of internet marketing for franchisors. Many franchisors are still pretty new at internet marketing; this gives new franchisors with strong internet marketing skills an advantage.

Not too many years ago, the "big boys," or well-known franchisors, had the advantage because they had far more money and resources to market their franchise opportunities. Back then, the marketing and media options were very expensive, and the new emerging franchisors were priced out of the competition. The internet has now leveled the playing field because the barriers of entry are lower, giving creativity, and not big marketing budgets, the advantage.

Consider the following benefits and tips when you develop your internet marketing efforts:

- *The internet allows an interactive experience.* Make sure your websites offer a personal experience to build value and trust. Include audio and video testimonials and introductions to your team. Make sure you hire a professional to create high-quality streaming media.

- *The internet generation is accustomed to immediate satisfaction.* Think how flustered you get when the computer takes more than a few seconds to open a page. Making sure the information that is most interesting to prospective franchise owners is easily accessible and loads quickly shows your technology competence to tech-savvy buyers.

- *The internet allows the prospective franchisee access to far more information than does an advertisement or brochure.* Your internet marketing should guide them down a discovery path that they can move through at their own pace.

WEBSITES

Website technology has evolved substantially over the last ten years. It is now relatively inexpensive to create and maintain a strong web presence. When websites became a product that everyone needed, thousands joined the ranks of "webmaster." The sad reality is the fact that there is no way for consumers to identify who is a true "master" and who may be a "disaster." Interview several web-design companies before making your selection. Also, check with their past clients to see how their sites are doing.

Here are some tips for creating a strong franchise website:

- Your site should have simple content and a clear call to action that is on the first page, visible without having to scroll down.

- Your site should be built on a search engine optimization (SEO)–friendly platform. Some of the older platforms can hurt your SEO rankings.

- Your site should be rich with keyword phrases—combinations of words that people enter into the search engines to find information. You can analyze the search terms that your prospects are using with a variety of online tools such as Google AdWords keyword tool. You may find that "dog grooming franchise" ranks higher than "pet grooming franchise." This enables you to use the more popular term on your site to rank higher for that phrase.

- Insert keywords in your titles, headings, and page titles.
- Include keywords in your URL (more commonly known as your web address) whenever possible. The address www.XYZfranchise.com may rank lower than www.XYZautorepairfranchise.com.
- Include a blog on your website and add new articles every week. Fresh, informative content will increase your site's ranking.
- Obtain "backlinks" from other websites in your industry. This is explored further in the upcoming "Blogs" section.
- Include social media icons (for Facebook, Twitter, LinkedIn, and so forth) that link directly to your social media pages.

EMAIL

Email is now commonplace. Email allows you to communicate much faster than traditional mail, now called snail mail. The following are some tips for your email efforts:

- Your email addresses should be connected to a dedicated URL. Rick@XYZautorepairfranchise.com is much better than XYZautorepairfranchise@freeemail.com.
- Include a "professional signature." It should contain your picture, logo, contact information, and social media links along with your name.
- Include a legal disclosure that specifies that your correspondence does not imply an offer to sell a franchise. Have a competent, experienced franchise attorney provide you with this language.
- Be sure to comply with the email rules when sending "email blast" campaigns, including opt-out options and approved recipients.
- Always return emails within 24 hours of receipt. Sooner is better.
- Have all company email messages proofread to ensure correct spelling, grammar, and punctuation are used.
- Be extra cautious when emailing from a smartphone—the typing is clumsy, and the spellcheck is notorious for changing words. Some businesspeople include an apology message for mistakes,

but this does not make the best impression.

BLOGS

You can think of blogs for your business in two ways. The first is the blog that should be a part of your website(s). You will want keyword-rich articles on your website blog to rank higher on organic searches. The second category is what some call the "blogosphere." There are thousands of great blog sites that already have tons of readership and rank high. You can submit your articles to these sites and include your website link. This creates a backlink, which increases your organic ranking and directs traffic to your site.

Blogs have enabled ordinary people the ability to publish their ideas and insights on the web for free. This reality has flooded the internet with content about every imaginable subject. Your company can gain exposure by submitting relevant articles to blogs that prospective franchisees may frequent. Apply the following tips for your blog efforts:

- Research your industry niche to find the top blog sites.
- Choose a specific keyword phrase for each article. Use it once in the title and once per 100 words. If you use it too many times in the article, though, it may be penalized by the search engines; 350 to 450 words is a good length for a blog article.
- Insert a link to your franchise website in each article.
- Make every article educational and newsworthy.
- Change at least 30 percent of the articles if you intend to submit them to more than one blog. The search engines will "de-dupe" or remove duplicate articles from rankings if they are exactly the same. You can buy software that assists you with the rewriting process.

WEB PRESENTATIONS

Technology has made meetings and presentations a snap. Not too many years ago, a meeting would require plane tickets, hotels, travel days, meals, and lost opportunity costs. Web presentations allow the presenter to share presentation slides, web content, audio and video testimonials, live presenter interactivity, and live two-way video.

Franchisors can now invite prospective franchisees to scheduled or impromptu web meetings to present their franchise opportunities. This is almost as effective as an in-person meeting, since you can cover the same information. You can meet with people all over the world from the convenience of your home or office. The following are some tips to consider when you launch your web presentations:

- You can sign up for web presentation options for a small monthly fee.
- Prepare a professional set of presentation slides and have them proofread. You may want to hire a consultant to develop this for you. This may be your first impression on prospects that are considering a huge investment.
- Always have the next step confirmed at the end of your presentation. Schedule the follow-up call, discovery day, or any other step when you are finished.
- Use this platform for franchise support and training as well. Connecting with your franchise owners is often the best way to keep you and your team engaged.

ELECTRONIC NEWSLETTERS (E-NEWSLETTERS)

Electronic newsletters can be very effective as long as you have an interested readership. You must have impactful and useful content to engage your readers. Newsletters have been used for decades, and most have little to no impact on their audience. Ask yourself when you last invested your time to read a newsletter.

> You must include "game-changing" and compelling ideas. What makes what you are writing so interesting? In today's world, there is an avalanche of information every day. Consider an interactive e-newsletter with links to actual solutions or informative articles.

SEARCH ENGINE OPTIMIZATION (SEO)

Search engine optimization has become a major part of businesses worldwide. SEO can be defined as any online efforts you make to drive traffic to your websites. Organic search results come from three primary elements of your website: fresh content, links, and keywords. You can target the most popular keyword and content based on your prospects' frequent search terms. You may want to hire a competent SEO consultant to help with this effort. They should offer a result guarantee for the keyword or keyword phrases that you choose to target.

SEARCH ENGINE MARKETING (SEM)

Search engine marketing or SEM is any effort to promote your business online. There are many companies that specialize in SEM that can assist you in your efforts. This will include SEO as well as pay options like pay-per-click advertising, banner advertisements, and other internet marketing.

Some of these options can be very targeted based on demographics and the audience's interests. You may notice when you log into your social media sites that the advertisements seem to match your interests. This form of behavioral marketing allows the advertiser to narrow the audience as they set up the campaign. You may even consider using *retargeting* or "follow ads" that appear, based on an individuals' interests and online habits, on the sites that the individual frequents. This technology enables targeted ads to "follow" a user based on their past browsing history. This creates the illusion that a certain brand is everywhere because the user sees the ad multiple times, in multiple places, as they browse.

SOCIAL MEDIA

Social media has changed the way people communicate. This platform enables people to create networks with friends, family, and business associates. The people within these networks can then keep track of each other and collectively communicate and have dialogue about anything that comes up, from very deep subjects to nonsense.

Social media has given people more direct access to influential individuals. Now, political figures and celebrities can post their thoughts dynamically as often as they want to their followers or fan base. This creates a more personal experience for many.

As a franchisor, you can have social media components that augment your other internet marketing efforts. Consider the following when you create your social media campaigns:

- Hire a professional to help you with this effort unless you are very familiar with social media. You will want to appoint someone within your company to focus on this to ensure consistency. Once you build a group of fans or followers, you must provide good information on a regular basis or you will lose them.

- Include great content to keep your audience engaged. Avoid posting "the fact of the day" type of postings just for the sake of posting something.

- Allow potential franchisees the ability to ask questions and get to know your company culture.

- Monitor the content carefully to make sure that it remains positive and professional.

Many franchisors today are facing the challenges of their franchisees launching their own social media campaigns. Social media can be a great marketing tool for franchise owners—if it is closely managed by the franchisor. The downside is the reality that it increases risk to your brand since outside individuals will comment on these platforms and become associated with your company. To promote appropriate social media use, apply the following to your franchisee social media program:

- Create a clear set of social media policies that give the franchisees very specific guidelines to adhere to. Include these policies in your operations manual and make sure that everyone understands and conforms accordingly.

- Consider hosting corporate-only social media platforms that link to the individual franchisee pages. Allow the franchise owners to post local articles, photos, and other relevant content to give them a local presence. This gives you the highest level of control.

- Appoint someone within your company to consistently monitor the content of all social media sites. This individual can also keep the sites current with interesting information. Many "spammers" and "trolls" target social media sites and can post offensive links and content. Be sure to block or eliminate these individuals from your sites.

- You will need more stringent policies and monitoring if you allow your franchise owners to manage their own social media efforts.

- Regardless of your final structure, you must be the clear leader for your franchise community when it comes to social media. Do not let it get away from you. It will be far more difficult to implement damage control years down the road than it will be to deal with these issues now.

- Include social media and other technology clauses along with your website references in your franchise disclosure document and franchise agreement.

TEXTING

Today, many of us rely on the instant response that comes from texting. Be prepared to have dynamic texting as a part of your franchise recruiting process. It is proven that people read and respond to text messages far more than email or even phone calls. You will want to offer texting as a communication option for prospective franchisees during the discovery process. You will also want to allow your franchisees texting options for support after they open for business.

PODCASTS

Podcasts are audio or video messages that can be featured on your website or emails. They are a good way to educate your prospective franchise owners as they move through your discovery process. You can break your franchise sales information into short high-impact audio or video segments. You can also optimize these for the search engines to drive traffic to your websites by posting them on all of the free sites and directing links back to your sites.

MOBILE APPS

Smartphones and tablets have changed the way we "do life." We now have fully functional computers in our pockets. Imagine combining an old-fashioned camera, video camera, desktop computer, GPS, music and book libraries, clock, time-management calendar, notebook, weather forecast, calculator, TV, and every game you can imagine in one small package that is smaller than a 1980s calculator.

New smart device applications, or *apps*, enter the marketplace daily. You will want to explore the available apps to identify possible options to promote your franchise opportunity. Depending on your business model, you may find the need to create your own app to connect your customers with the services of your franchise owners. Hire a company that has a good track record to create your custom apps.

TELEVISION COMMERCIALS AND INTERACTIVE TV

Technology has made television more affordable with cable and network options that allow local commercial customization. TV ads on network television stations once were very costly, which made them unaffordable for most small businesses. However, today you can advertise your franchise opportunity by placing commercials in key markets and targeted channels at a fraction of the cost of prior years. In some markets you can add the option for an interactive, immediate response. This option allows viewers to request more information by pressing a button on their remote control immediately, which is when they are most interested in the offer.

FUTURE TECHNOLOGIES

Some say that a majority of the technology that we will be using ten years from now has not even been invented yet. It sounds crazy, but is not hard to imagine when you consider what the first cell phone looked like. If you ever called someone from your car phone and said, "You will never guess where I am calling you from," then you get this.

How Do I Compete?

You may ask yourself this question when you consider the thousands of franchise opportunities available around the world. Some of them are

> Commit to staying ahead of your competition when it comes to technology. This can be the deciding factor for many businesses. Listen to your advisors and franchise owners as they experience challenges in the field. Be willing to innovate and push the envelope as technology evolves. Some who choose to stick to the good old-fashioned basics evaporate because they can't keep up. Be the leader!

industry giants with huge marketing budgets. This can seem daunting as you consider entering the franchise world as a new, small company. The truth of the matter is there has never been a better time to throw your hat in the ring! The playing field is now level. You don't need a million-dollar marketing budget to be successful. With technology on your side, you can get your message out to the world by being creative and persistent.

Consider the following tips:

- *Hire experts—you don't know what you don't know.* An experienced franchise development consultant and franchise attorney will save you tons of money and grief.
- *Create a solid marketing plan.* Use this book to outline your marketing and recruiting program to ensure that you are covering all the bases.
- *Commit to your plan and execute it* (no matter what).
- *When you have success, tell the world.*
- Take the time to build relationships with your franchise owners. Your first franchisees "buy in" because they trust you and believe in you.

- *Include the first franchise owners in the "big picture success story."* Make them part of your owners advisory committee and let them help you solve problems and create new programs.
- *Offer funding alternatives.* Become the "rainmaker" by offering financing and investment alternatives to standard bank loans. In today's world, people are buying franchises with creative solutions like self-directed 401(k)s, investor pools, angel investors, and even government programs like the EB5 international investor option.

Conclusion

The American dream has always been based on the reality that citizens have the opportunity to achieve successful business enterprise in a free market. We have the privilege to cultivate good ideas, products, systems, and methods for delivering products and services and then turn them into businesses.

You wake up at two in the morning with a groundbreaking epiphany. You sit at the kitchen table with a stack of blank paper and a pen. Your brilliance pours onto the paper, and in short order you have created a business model that has never been done before.

You go online and form a corporation or LLC in minutes. You create a website. You start making money, build a great business, and franchise to expand and share your brilliance with others.

America is the birthplace of innovation and franchising. You have the best opportunity right in front of you. Invest in something you can really believe in—yourself and the opportunity of a lifetime!

CHAPTER 15

Final Thoughts on Franchising Your Business

Franchising your business is a multifaceted decision, as you can see. The process does not have to be difficult and expensive as long as you have a well-planned franchising roadmap and realistic expectations. Franchising your business can also be very lucrative as you take your already successful business model and duplicate it to build a thriving enterprise that can be worth big money in the future. This chapter will give you some final considerations as you get ready to choose the road for expanding your business.

Can You Afford the Franchising Process?

Franchising your business does not have to be terribly costly if you budget correctly and have a game plan. You don't want to waste money unnecessarily or spend money that can be differed until you have revenue coming in from franchise sales.

You should be able to get a pretty good idea of the project costs when you interview franchise attorneys and franchise development consultants. Be sure you are talking to experienced individuals who have active franchise practices. Standard business (and not franchise-specific) advisors can lead you down the wrong path or dissuade you from franchising due to their lack of experience or comfort with franchising. The franchise industry is very unique and has many elements that may not align with general business models, so choose your consultants and advisors wisely.

Impounds and Deferred Fee-Collection Stipulations

If you are in a registration state and the attorney for the state examining your application for franchising determines you do not have sufficient capitalization to open the franchises you plan to open, the applicable state agency may still grant you a permit to sell franchises. To do this, however, you must open an impound account in a bank chartered in that particular state for the direct deposit of all franchise fees. In essence, an impound is a trust account: The franchisor is required to have the franchisee write a check to the designated depository bank, to be held in trust until the franchisee provides a written declaration to the registration state that his or her franchise is open and that the franchisor has performed all of their opening obligations under the franchise agreement.

Once this declaration is received, it is filed with the appropriate state registration agency; if the agency approves the declaration, it will prepare an order allowing the franchisor to remove the franchisee's funds from the bank. The franchisor then submits this order to the bank, and the bank pays that particular franchise fee to the franchisor.

Unfortunately, not too many banks are familiar with these trust account procedures, and most escrow accounts are extremely expensive—$1,000 to $2,000 in some cities for each franchisee escrow account. In some instances, your franchise attorney may be able to convince the state authority that you will provide in your franchise agreement that you will defer, or not require payment of, the initial franchise fee until the franchisee has opened his or her store and advised you that he or she agrees you have fulfilled all your opening obligations under the franchise agreement. Many registration states will allow this type of provision in lieu of impounds.

> You will want to budget for this to make sure you are prepared to get those franchise owners through training and open without having their respective franchise fees in your bank. Remember that this only applies to a handful of registration states and is not applicable in any of the 35 non-registration states, so factor this in to your registration-state strategy.

Multistate Franchise Taxes and Accounting

You will want to interview accounting firms that have an active franchise practice just like the attorneys and franchise-development consultants mentioned earlier. Discuss the various business entity types and corresponding advantages and disadvantages so you set it up right the first time.

You also want to talk to them about taxes in your home state as well as other states that you will be doing business in as a national franchisor. They naturally will advise you on your federal taxes as well. Set this up from the very beginning so you don't have to change things after the fact, which can cost you dearly.

Presently, franchise income has generally been held not to be passive income if the franchisor has ongoing responsibilities. In addition, the Internal Revenue Service places certain restrictions on when the franchisor can report income as earned. Generally, the franchisor can report the franchise fee as earned only during the time the franchise is operating. Since you will need annual audited statements, your CPA (required) will advise you of the current tax regulations on these tax matters.

Franchise Associations and Advertising Councils

Most registration states have laws that prohibit a franchisor from interfering with the right of franchisees to have their own associations. Franchisees can have an association, but it is in your best interest as a franchisor to form that association, and you should be involved in its operations. Generally, a franchisee association will not be formed until seven to ten franchisees are operating in a given area.

A franchisee association should be an advisory body only, since you, as the franchisor, should still determine the specific procedures to be followed by the franchise system. Many successful franchisors, including McDonald's, have improved their systems by implementing suggestions from franchisees and making changes within the entire system after they have been proven successful at one or two test-franchise operations.

Like franchisee associations, franchisee advertising councils can be effective, too. Each franchisee usually has their own idea of what the ideal advertising media should be—and most of the ideas are cost-prohibitive. For instance, almost all franchisees want local, regional, and national television exposure, which is much too costly in most cases and clearly in excess of the advertising fund fees collected from franchisees. It would be better to poll the franchisees from time to time in order to get an idea of which local advertising media they have found effective in their operations.

A good franchise agreement should compel the franchisee to provide written reports of all types, particularly covering sales data, and this information could then be compiled into meaningful results for each franchisee in the system. This is one of the major benefits of the franchise system—the experiences of each franchisee, rather than his or her theories, can be compiled, analyzed, and passed on for the benefit of the entire system.

Franchise Discovery Process

Good franchise owners tend to be people that can follow a system. Due to this reality, it is a good practice to create a step-by-step discovery process for prospective owners to follow. This allows them to learn as they go, which is more effective than trying to absorb all of the information at one time. This also enables you to track their progress and commitment level as they move through the steps.

FRANCHISE BROCHURE

Following a prospective franchisee's initial inquiry, you should send them an informational brochure. Brochures can cost anywhere from a few dollars to thousands of dollars to prepare. Depending on your personal taste and budget, it may be preferable to use a simple franchise brochure stating many of the items that are in the disclosure, featuring a nice overview of the attributes of the particular franchise system.

In California and a few other states where registration is necessary, the brochure, like any advertisement, must be submitted to the appropriate registration authority for prior approval. An ad is generally required to be submitted in duplicate anywhere from three to seven days before publication, with a duty upon the agency to disapprove it within such time or the ad is deemed approved.

FRANCHISE CANDIDATE APPLICATION

In addition to sending a brochure, you should make an attempt to find out if the franchisee is financially qualified to buy a franchise. Therefore, the first document forwarded to the franchisee should be a franchise application seeking the franchisee's background information and net worth. This application should be tailored to your needs and reviewed by your legal counsel.

FRANCHISE DISCLOSURE DOCUMENTS AND RECEIPT

After a prospective franchisee has completed the background application and net worth financial form, use the document to assess their suitability to your franchise by checking out every disclosure that you can. If you determine a franchisee to have the necessary qualifications, the next step is to forward your disclosure document to the prospective franchisee or meet with him or her and present the franchise disclosure document. The prospect acknowledges receiving the disclosure by signing a document called a *receipt* and returning it to you, the franchisor. You will find an example of a receipt at the end of online at www.franchisebiblestudy.com.

Always prepare two receipt forms—one copy for the prospective franchisee to keep and the other to sign and return to you. If the franchisee signs one and returns it to you but doesn't retain a copy for his or her own records, at some time in the future, particularly if the situation involves legal proceedings, they may contend that they didn't receive the disclosure in a timely manner as dictated by the current rule. This initial accusation might be avoided if you provide the franchisee with a copy of his or her acknowledgment receipt at the time it is executed.

It is a good practice to provide the potential franchisee with the required disclosure document before any discussion about it.

If the franchisee is out of state and the franchise is to be operated in your registration state, the disclosure document to be sent to the prospective franchisee would be your in-state disclosure document. However, if the franchise is to be operated in another state, you will be required to register in the other state before offering your franchise.

You will find a suggested discovery process outline in the Franchise Your Business tab of the *Franchise Bible* Study (www.franchisebiblestudy. com).

Avoiding Litigation and Arbitration

Avoid litigation if at all possible, of course. Not only is litigation expensive—although less so if an arbitration provision is included—but the facts of the litigation or arbitration must be reported in the franchise disclosure document. This includes furnishing the name, address, and phone number of each litigating franchisee. It also makes marketing future franchises much more difficult, since prospective franchisees can contact the listed litigating franchisees and, in all probability, will receive negative information about the franchise operation.

BREACH OF CONTRACT

Some registration states provide that if a franchisor fails to properly register a disclosure document, the franchisee can automatically file an action for rescission and get his or her money back. However, many other states merely make this a possible criminal violation while upholding the validity of the franchise agreement. The general rules of agreement regarding substantial breach would then apply—that is, a franchisee would have the burden to prove to a judge, jury, or arbitrator that the franchisor made a specific written commitment and failed to follow through on that commitment. If this were proved, it would constitute a substantial breach of the franchise agreement. There is a fine line between a "substantial" breach and an "insubstantial" breach, wherein a verdict for rescission would not be granted, but rather a judgment for whatever money damages the franchisee may have proven. In addition, most franchisors, in their franchise agreements, present a minimum amount of written obligations that apply after the franchisee has opened his or her operation.

If you are proven to have committed a fraud—making fraudulent promises that were not true that induced the franchisee to enter into the franchise agreement—they may seek to rescind the agreement based on what is called *common-law fraud*. It is not the purpose of this book to be a franchise legal manual; therefore, you must take every precaution to make sure your employees, particularly your franchise salespeople, make no representations that are not set forth in the written disclosure document. In addition, actively abide by all after-opening obligations to the franchisee, as provided in the franchise agreement.

PROS AND CONS OF ARBITRATION

The positive aspect of arbitration is that you can generally select an arbitrator who has a firm knowledge of franchising from the standpoints of both franchisor and franchisee, as opposed to a judge or jury who know little, if anything, about franchising. The ideal arbitrator is one who has a legal and a franchising background, because arbitrators who are businesspeople tend to give both parties some type of award. Therefore, neither party wins. As a straight legal rule in the judicial system, if a contract is breached or a franchisee has been defrauded, only one party should win, and the other party should get nothing. In a major arbitration, three arbitrators may be selected, so as to eliminate the chance of selecting a totally outrageous sole arbitrator who will render a bad decision.

The negative side of arbitration is that it is final and binding, and, in most cases, the decision cannot be appealed. However, most court appeals are won by the party that won at the lower level. In addition, court appeals are extremely expensive and time-consuming.

Franchise Fees, Royalties, and Other Fees

Many franchisors fail because they expect to immediately profit by charging high initial franchise fees, high royalty fees, and high advertising fees. However, if you look at what is happening in the American market, you will find that discounters who charge lower fees and bank on volume to make profits have overtaken the retail market. Most franchisees cannot handle high initial franchise fees and even higher royalty fees based on their gross sales. So, keep your expenses to a minimum while maintaining a high level of services to the franchisee. The franchisee is the marketing arm of the franchisor; if the franchisor can set up a franchisee by breaking even, he or she has already accomplished a great feat.

> Having 1,000 franchisees paying 6 percent of revenue is much more profitable than having 100 franchisees paying 8 percent.

Many franchisors who set their fees higher are unable to sell many franchises—and the franchises they sell have such high fees that they soon go out of business. In some states where franchisees have brought lawsuits against franchisors with excessive fees and royalties, the courts have sided with the franchisees.

Always make detailed projections regarding how much profit you can make with a minimum amount of franchise fees and royalties, taking into consideration the profit you will make from the sale of your products and services to your franchisees. It will be time well spent.

Making the Decision to Franchise

Now that you are more familiar with franchising in general, you are better prepared to make your final decision. Be sure to consider whether the following things are true:

- The advantages of franchising outweigh the disadvantages.
- Your business has a market and a trademark that is or can be registered.
- Your current personnel or outside consulting personnel familiar with franchising are well qualified and available.
- You have no problem with selecting sites or preparing the manual.
- You have the working capital necessary to start the franchising process.
- You have sufficient capital to market your franchise.
- You have prepared a realistic business plan and budget for your franchise entity.
- You have an attorney who is not only experienced in franchise law but also familiar with the business aspects of franchising and the necessary relationship with the franchisee.

If these statements apply to you, you are ready to move ahead to a new way of conducting business and an exciting way of life.

Conclusion

Franchising your business can enable you and your business team to grow your business concept on a very large scale. It can be very rewarding to see others thrive through your business. Teaching others how to become successful business owners has a ripple effect that touches many.

PART III

Franchise Ten Commandments: Thou Shalt Thrive!

The Franchise Ten Commandments was created to help both existing franchisors and franchise owners thrive. This section contains tried-and-true tips and techniques that have been the framework for countless franchise success stories.

Franchisor's Ten Commandments

Franchisors often get off to a good start only to find themselves hitting a dry spell that we call the *franchise doldrums* (usually occurring between 11 and 24 franchise units). This can happen when the momentum of the first wave of "inner circle" franchise buyers ends. Apply the following to make your franchise organization thrive:

I. *Get your "master's degree in franchising."* Even though you are an expert in your field of business, turning your business into a franchise model is starting a whole new business. You will find many educational options online at www.franchisebiblestudy.com to enable you to become a master of the franchise industry.

II. *Be an inspirational leader.* Your most important role as the leader of your franchise company is that of inspiration. Your franchise community will look to you for your vision and guidance. Never lose sight of the importance of your position as the visionary leader. This is the starting point for building a large successful organization.

III. *Build an executive and support team of believers.* As you grow, you are going to bring more talent to your corporate team. Choose wisely and make sure you hire based on the most qualified people for the job. Also make sure that everyone on your team is a believer in your systems and culture and has a true commitment to the success of the franchise community.

IV. *Commit to creating the appropriate infrastructure.* You will want to implement a balanced approach to your infrastructure building. Take on too much, too fast, and you can go broke. Too little, too late may result in your franchisees failing. Get the specialized outside consultants to help you with this critical strategy.

V. *Don't allow things to fall through the cracks.* It is not uncommon to see new franchisors neglect attention to detail as they move through the first few years. This occurs for a variety of reasons, including lack of experience, operating short-staffed, and the overall absence of functional tracking systems. Growing too fast has its ups and downs as well. Paying attention to detail and implementing systems and policies from the very beginning are essential.

VI. *Apply the upside-down pyramid strategy.* Some franchise organizations have tried to grow using the traditional management model that they were accustomed to as an employer with employees. Franchise owners of course are not employees, and the servant attitude that the upside-down pyramid structure offers in turn will make your franchise organization much more profitable and successful.

VII. *Apply the Three Franchise Decision Lens Philosophy.* Many franchise organizations have suffered the fallout of bad decisions that could have easily been avoided if they simply considered the legal, political, and practical aspects of the decision and the impact it would have on the franchise community—and in turn, the overall franchise organization.

VIII. *Form and host your franchise owner's advisory committee.* The best way to make sure you are aligned with your franchise owners is to form and host an effective owner's advisory committee. A well-run committee can act as a rudder to help you steer your organization.

IX. *Plan and host your annual franchise convention.*

X. *Implement your franchise incentive and rewards program.*

Depending on the current size of your company, you may have some of these systems in place and may only want to update, fine-tune, or revise for your business model. We have found these to be the most impactful elements of a successful franchise organization. You will find resources to learn more and tools to implement the Franchise Ten Commandments at www.franchisebiblestudy.com.

Franchise Owner's Ten Commandments

Some people buy a franchise with the belief that it is easy or that the franchisor is going to make them successful. The franchisor has gone through a lot of preparation, work, and expense to create a franchise model that you can join and achieve your own success story with. Many people have become very successful and extremely wealthy through franchise ownership, but it is largely up to you to make it happen.

You can implement the following to make the most of your opportunity as a franchise owner:

I. *Get your master's degree in franchising.* Even though your franchisor trains and supports you to gain a level of expertise in your field of business, growing that into a thriving franchise company takes an education in franchising. You will find many educational options offered online at www.franchisebiblestudy.com to enable you to become a master of the franchise industry.

II. *Identify opportunities to be a part of the franchisor's growth.* Historically the most involved franchise owners tend to be among the most successful. Your first priority is to run your business, of course, but you may find synergies with the franchisor that can help you learn more about the business and also benefit the franchisor.

III. *Strive to be the top producing franchise owner.* Some say that the first step to becoming the top producer is simply believing that you can be the top producer. You made a huge investment of your time and money to join the franchise system, so you may as well endeavor to achieve the highest return on investment possible. Hint: The top producer common denominator found across most industries is simply the franchisees that make the commitment to religiously follow the franchise system.

IV. *Be a leader in the franchise owner community.* Remember how important it was for you to look up to the leadership of more experienced and successful franchise owners when you first joined the system? A wildly successful franchisor and franchise community will help you make your franchise more successful. Don't be afraid to seek to become a leader among the franchisees to help them achieve their goals and dreams.

V. *Be a mentor.* Some franchisors have formal mentorship programs in place. Teaching is the best way to learn in most cases. Again, the overall health of the entire franchise network has a huge impact on each and every individual in the organization, so it pays to mentor other owners in more ways than one.

VI. *Volunteer to serve on the owner's advisory committee.* The owner's advisory committee for your franchise may offer an opportunity for you to participate. This may allow you to gather feedback, ideas, and concerns from other franchisees in your region and communicate to the corporate headquarters, or attend regular meetings to make suggestions to influence the direction the company takes in the future.

VII. *Be an innovator.* You are in the trenches every day and may create a tool or process that makes your business better. Be sure to take your new ideas through the proper channels with your franchisor so the entire community can benefit.

VIII. *Be a contributor, not a consumer.* Be a part of the businesses "big picture" instead of standing on the sidelines. Contribute your genius and experience and lend a hand whenever you can.

IX. *Participate in the annual convention.* The annual convention has always been our favorite event of the year. Since you are a member of a "party" and not so much a team, you rarely get to be on the same playing field together. Make the most of the conventions and pitch in if possible.

X. *Build your enterprise and legacy through multi-unit ownership.* Some of the most successful and wealthiest business owners we know are multi-unit franchisees. Once you have proven to yourself and your franchisor that you have what it takes to launch, grow, and thrive with one franchise, it may be time to add more units.

Franchise ownership is an exciting business model. We have evaluated countless franchise models over more than 20 years in the franchise industry and have found these practices to be the "secret sauce" for successful franchise ownership. You will find resources to learn more and tools to implement the Franchise Ten Commandments at www.franchisebiblestudy.com.

Conclusion

It has been said that you only get out of life what you put in to it. Your business journey has the potential to take you to great places. We hope you will find that the *Franchise Bible* is a valuable roadmap to franchise success.

Franchise Bible Study
Franchise Bible Accompaniment Online Study Guide
www.franchisebiblestudy.com

Franchise Hub Center
Franchise Accelerator Facility
5231 South Quebec Street
Greenwood Village, Colorado 80111
www.myfranchisehub.com

Vet Starter® Military
Military Veteran Franchise Ownership Resources
www.vetstarter.com

International Franchise Association
www.franchise.org
1900 K Street, N.W., Suite 700
Washington, DC 20006
Phone: (202) 628-8000
Fax: (202) 628-0812
Small Business Administration (SBA) Franchise Registry
www.franchiseregistry.com
franchiseregistry@frandata.com
(800) 485-9570

Entrepreneur.com

Find franchise opportunities and small business franchises for sale.
Includes franchising costs, fees, training, and rankings information online.
http://www.entrepreneur.com

Entrepreneur's Franchise 500®

Annual ranking of America's top franchise opportunities
http://www.entrepreneur.com/franchise500/index.html

Franchise Nomenclature

Like so many niche businesses, franchising has a language all its own. Here are definitions for many:

ACH or Automated Clearing House refers to the process used for electronic bank-to-bank transfers of fees due to Franchisor. This means that the Franchisor can automatically withdraw funds from your account to pay for such items as Royalties and advertising fees.

Affiliates means an entity controlled by, controlling, or under common control with another entity. Affiliates are sometimes called "sister" companies.

Arbitration is an alternative dispute resolution mechanism that replaces a state or federal court. In arbitration an "arbitrator" or "arbiter" (acting as a private judge) is called upon to resolve a legal claim between the Franchisor and Franchisee. The decision of the arbitrator is as binding on the parties to the disputes as would be the decision by a court of law.

Area Developer means a person or business entity that agrees as a Franchisee to open multiple franchised businesses within a certain development area.

The Area Developer signs a Franchise Agreement with the Franchisor, and then owns and operates each unit developed under the agreement.

Area Representative or Regional Developer means any person or business entity given the right by the Franchisor to locate potential Franchisees (who then sign the franchise agreement with the Franchisor) and/or to whom the Area Representative will provide some or all of the services otherwise required to be delivered by the Franchisor.

Competitive Business is a term used in defining the terms of a Noncompetition Covenant (defined below). To be enforceable any noncompetition covenant must be reasonably limited in its scope. Here, the identity of a competitive business must be reasonably close to the identity of the franchised business you bought. For instance, it is fair for a pizza franchise to deny you the right to compete against it with another pizza business. It would be unfair for the Franchisor however to deny you the right to compete against it with for instance, a burger joint.

Computer System means the computer hardware and software that the Franchisor requires you to have to operate the franchised business.

Compliance refers to the minimum standards you must meet to remain a Franchisee. Compliance requires that you follow the system described by the Franchisor and that you make all payments to Franchisor on a timely basis. Sometimes the Franchisor will deem you to be out of compliance if you have breached the Franchise Agreement "x" number of times in a 12-month period even though you may have timely cured each such violation. In such a case, the Franchisor may terminate your franchise rights because you fell out of Compliance.

Cure means the right that you have to fix a breach of the Franchise Agreement. For instance, if you fail to follow a certain rule or regulation, the Franchisor may send you a notice of default which will say something to the effect that you have breached the Franchise Agreement by failing to follow a stated rule and which says that you have "x" number of days to fix or "cure" the breach by again following the rule. Most Franchise Agreements have Events of Default (see below) that can be cured and some that cannot be cured.

Default Notice means the notice that the Franchisor will send the Franchisee if Franchisee breaches any covenant of the Franchise Agreement.

Designated Manager refers to the person besides the owner of the franchise that has received the Franchisor's training and who can operate the franchised business in the absence of the owner. This person may be identified by another title in a Franchise Agreement. The meaning however will be the same.

Due Date usually means the date on which Royalties and other fees are due to Franchisor and is the date that the Franchisor will automatically take money from your operating account through the ACH process.

Financial Performance Representation or Earnings Claim is any oral, visual, or written representation made by the Franchisor to a prospective Franchisee that states or implies any specific level or potential for any sales, earnings, profits, or similar financial gain that could be realized by the Franchisee. Franchisors can make such representations ONLY if the information is disclosed in Item 19 of the disclosure portion of the FDD.

Effective Date usually means the date that the Franchise Agreement was fully executed by the Franchisor and Franchisee.

Event of Default refers to any of a list of breaches defined in the Franchise Agreement. For instance, an Event of Default would be your failure to follow the system. This could be because an employee failed to wear a uniform or because you failed to deliver the quality of product or service required under the Franchise Agreement.

Exclusive Territory is a franchise term of art and means that the Franchisor is giving you a certain geographic area in which you (and no other Franchisee) can sell the franchised goods or services. An Exclusive Territory could be as small as a city block or as large as an entire city, county, or state. Some franchise systems offer Exclusive Territories while others do not. By law, if the Franchisor offers no Exclusive Territory it must state the following in Item 12 of the Franchise Disclosure Document:

"You will not receive an exclusive territory. You may face competition from other Franchisees, from outlets that we own, or from other channels of distribution or competitive brands that we control."

Expiration of Franchise Agreement means the date on which the term of the franchise agreement ends. For instance, if the term of the franchise agreement is 10 years, it expires on the last day of the ten-year period. Compare this to "Termination."

Fair Market Value means the value that a reasonable person who is under no duress or obligation to buy, would pay to a seller who is under no duress or obligation to sell. In the franchise setting, this measure is often used when valuing the Franchisee's interest in his furniture, fixtures, and equipment, and the value of the Franchisee's interest in the franchise itself. As is often the case, the buyer and seller may not agree on the Fair Market Value, and as a result, most Franchise Agreements will provide a mechanism to resolve the impasse through the use of an independent and disinterest appraiser. As is most often the case, the goodwill of the business attributable to the Franchisor's Marks will not be valued because it belongs to the Franchisor and is not "owned" by the Franchisee.

Federal Trade Commission is the governmental authority that regulates franchising on a national level. The FTC (with the help of the North American Securities Administrators Association the "NASAA") dictates the content of the FDD.

Force Majeure refers to so-called "acts of god" or other matters of which you have no reasonable control. In most Franchise Agreements, an event of Force Majeure usually excuses both the Franchisor and Franchisee from performing certain obligations until the event has passed. Many times Force Majeure will NOT excuse a Franchisee from making monetary payments. If you cannot offer a certain service or good because of serious weather, you will be excused from what otherwise would be an Event of Default until the weather has cleared up.

Franchise means ". . . any continuing commercial relationship or arrangement, whatever it may be called, in which the terms of the offer or contract specify, or the franchise seller promises or represents, orally or in writing, that:

1. The franchisee will obtain the right to operate a business that is identified or associated with the franchisor's trade mark, or to offer, sell, or distribute goods, services, or commodities that are identified or associated with the franchisor's trade mark;

2. The franchisor will exert or has authority to exert a significant degree of control over the franchisee's method of operation, or provide significant assistance in the franchisee's method of operation; and

3. As a condition of obtaining or commencing operation of the franchise, the franchisee makes a required payment or commits to make a required payment to the franchisor or its affiliate." 16 Code of Federal Regulations, Section 436.1(h) (2007).

Franchise Agreement means the actual contract between the Franchisor and you. The "FDD" (as defined below) is NOT a contract. Instead, it is a federally mandated disclosure document that contains an exact copy of the Franchise Agreement, and of all other agreements that the Franchisor may require you to sign.

Franchisee means the person or business entity that is granted the right to operate the franchised business. The Franchisee may be a natural person though most often the Franchisee is a business entity (e.g. a corporation or a limited liability company). If Franchisee is a business entity, the definition may also include all of Franchisee's directors, officers, shareholders, members, managers, and partners. In addition if the Franchisee is a business entity, the Franchisor will often demand that one or more of the officers, directors, shareholders, members, managers, and partners sign a guaranty, which in turns states that each such person is equally responsible for the performance of the Franchisee under Franchise Agreement.

Franchise Disclosure Document or FDD means the disclosure document required by the Federal Trade Commission to be delivered to you at least 14 calendar days before you sign any agreement or pay any money to the Franchisor. The FDD contains several parts. The first part of the FDD is the disclosure portion that comprises 23 "Items." The FTC dictates that all Franchisors offering a franchise in the United States MUST follow the exact same format when drafting the disclosure portion of the FDD. The disclosure portion is then followed by other mandatory disclosures including the Franchise Agreement and any other documents you will be required to sign.

Franchisee Manual or Manual means the operations manuals (that may be more than one manual, booklet, or handout), that will be delivered to you before you open for business. The Manuals usually explain how to operate the business and include topics on such matters as accounting, customer service, preparation of goods to be delivered to the customer (e.g., the way to cook a burger), quality control, and the like.

Franchisee National Advertising Fee or National Advertising Fee means the fee usually collected by the Franchisor to be used to create a national advertising campaign around the franchised product or services.

Franchisor means the person or entity identified as the Franchisor. It usually includes not only the Franchisor's business entity, but also the Franchisor's predecessors, any Affiliate, or any parent and each such business entity's shareholders, directors, officers, managers, members, employees, and agents, and all successors, and assignees.

Grand Opening means the celebration you fund at the time of the opening of your franchised business. The Grand Opening Cost is the amount you spend on your Grand Opening.

Indemnification means you agree to pay the Franchisor for any loss the Franchisor suffers because of your breach of the Franchise Agreement. For instance, if you injure a customer and if the customer sues you and the Franchisor, you agree to cover not only your legal costs and losses but also those of the Franchisor.

Initial Franchise Fee and IFF means the fee you pay the Franchisor for the award to you of the Franchise Agreement.

Initial Term means the number of years from the Effective Date of the Franchise Agreement to the last day of the Franchise Agreement. The Initial Term may be a length of time from a few years to a decade or longer. The Initial Term does not refer to any renewal or extension that may be granted. Such additional term is often called the "Renewal Term" "Successor Franchise Term," or words to that effect.

Late Fee means the fee that the Franchisor may charge for your failure to timely make payments. If the ACH method is used, you may incur a Late

Fee if there is not enough money in your account to pay what is owed to the Franchisor.

License in the franchise setting means the right granted to the Franchisee by the Franchisor to use the Franchisor's trademarks, trade names, logos, and other intellectual property. All franchise agreements are licenses, but all licenses are not franchises.

Local Advertising Fee or words to that effect refers to the minimum amount of money that the Franchisor may require you to spend on advertising in your Exclusive Territory or in your local market.

North American Securities Administrators Association, Inc. or NASAA is the group of state securities regulators that work with the FTC to create rules, regulations, and guidelines that control many aspects of the franchise industry. For instance, the format of the FDD and the guidelines for creating the FDD have been drafted by the NASAA.

Noncompetition Covenant is a part of the Franchise Agreement that states that you may not invest in, or work in a Competitive Business. Since such covenants seek to deny you the right to work in a certain industry, virtually all of the states will strictly construe this covenant against the Franchisor. Indeed, in some states such as California, such covenants are deemed unenforceable. To be enforceable at all, covenant must be reasonable in its definition of a Competitive business, in the time period during which you are denied the right to participate in a competitive business, and in the identity of geographic area in which you are denied the right to compete. If you operate a restaurant, a reasonable covenant may for a period of between 6 months and five years prohibit you from operating a similar restaurant (being one that serves the same type of food in the same type of atmosphere) within your Exclusive Territory (if one was given to you), within the Exclusive Territory of another Franchisee or company-owned restaurant, or with "x" miles of the perimeter of any such Exclusive Territory.

Opening Period means the date by which you must be open for business.

Principal Operator means the person authorized by the business-entity Franchisee to receive the Franchisor's training, to operate the franchised business, and to act as the contact between Franchisor and Franchisee. For instance, if the Franchisee is a corporation, the Principal Operator may be its president.

Proprietary Information, Confidential Information, Trade Secret Information or words to that effect refers to the secrets of the Franchisor that make its franchise unique and different. It often includes all of the Marks, the Manuals, the training methods and materials delivered to you, recipes, and financial aspects of the business. This information is never to be shared with anyone except employees and then only if he or she needs the information to perform his or her work.

Reasonable Business Judgment refers to the standard that a Franchisor will use to evaluate changes to the system, requests made by you to deviate from the system, or to determine whether to offer you renewal rights. Often use of the Franchisor's Reasonable Business Judgment will mean that Franchisor's determination on a matter will prevail even where other alternatives are also reasonable if Franchisor is intending to benefit, or are acting in a way that could reasonably benefit any component of the System and/or the Marks, any one or more of the Franchisees, or any other aspect of the franchise system. Such decisions may include, but will not be limited to, decisions that may: enhance and/or protect the Marks and the System; increase Student satisfaction; increase the use of the services all Franchisees offer; and matters that correspond with Franchisee satisfaction. Franchisor will not be required to consider any Franchisee's particular economic or other circumstances when exercising our Reasonable Business Judgment. Reasonable Business Judgment decisions will not affect all Franchisees equally, and some may benefit while others will not.

Registration States refers to that states those require the Franchisor to have the FDD reviewed and approved by state authorities prior to selling in that state, states that require yearly notification filings with the state to affirm that Franchisor is selling in the state, and states that require Franchisor to file for an exemption. The Registration States are: California, Hawaii, Illinois, Indiana, Maryland, Michigan, Minnesota, North Dakota, New York, Oregon, Rhode Island, South Dakota, Virginia, Washington, and Wisconsin. Florida, Kentucky, Nebraska, Texas, and Utah require some form of registration or exemption filing. In the Registration States, the Franchisor must amend the FDD to conform to the state's rules or regulations.

Royalty means either a flat fee charged by the Franchisor for each transaction done through your franchised business, or means a percentage of your revenue (most often a percentage of your Gross Revenue). Royalties can range from 1 to 10 percent or more. Royalties are an ongoing revenue stream for the Franchisor and is one area in which Franchisors must compete with other franchise opportunities.

Subfranchisee means the person or entity that is sold a franchise opportunity by a Subfranchisor. The subfranchisee thus has a contract not between the Franchisor and the franchisee, but instead has a contract between the Subfranchisor (who has stepped into the shoes of the Franchisor) and the Franchisee (now called the Subfranchisee).

Subfranchisor means the person or business entity that is granted the right by the Franchisor to sell franchises under Subfranchisor's signature in a defined geographic area. The Subfranchisor in the past has been called a "Master Franchisee." In this arrangement, the Subfranchisor steps into the shoes of the Franchisor by locating prospective Franchisees, by signing the franchise agreement as the franchisor, and by performing all of the duties of the Franchisor. These arrangements are most often seen where the Franchisor sells opportunities internationally or where the Franchisor grants subfranchise rights to a person or entity that will operate in one or more states.

Successor Franchise Fee or Renewal Fee means the fee that the Franchisor may charge when you seek to renew the franchise at the end of the Initial Term.

Successor Franchise Term means the number of years that the renewal lasts. It may be a term equal to the Initial Term or it may be a shorter period.

System means the Franchisor's manner and method without limitation: the manner and method of training delivered to the Franchisee; the operations, standards, and procedures the Franchisee will use in the day-to-day operation of the franchised business; the advertising programs to be used in promoting the franchised business; the economic and financial characteristics of the Franchised Business; any Proprietary Information owned by Franchisor; any of its Marks; and all other copyrighted, trade secret, or confidential information.

Term means the length of the franchise agreement. This is expressed in years and can be as short as three to five years, or it can be ten years or longer.

Termination means that the franchise agreement has ended on a date earlier than the Expiration date. Termination usually occurs because of breach by the franchisee of the franchise agreement.

Trademarks or Marks means all trademarks, trade names, logos, service marks, and similar commercial symbols that the Franchisor requires you to use in identifying your franchised business. In virtually all cases, the Franchisor will have a trademark registered with the United States Patent and Trademark Office (USPTO). The presence (or absence) of this registration is found at Item 13 of the disclosure portion of the FDD.

Trade Name means the name under which a business chooses to operate.

Training refers to the training that the Franchisor gives you before you open for business. Training must be defined in detail in Item 11 of the disclosure portion of the FDD.

Transfer means the act of transferring your interest in the franchised business, your interest in the assets of the franchise, or your interest in the business entity that owns the franchise rights to another person or entity. Transfers usually include transfers that are made by gift, by order of a court (as in a divorce or bankruptcy), and in most situations where the Franchisee seeks to divest himself of a material interest in the franchise, its assets, or the business. Transfers are almost always strictly controlled by the Franchisor.

Transfer Fee is the fee that most Franchisor's charge at the time of the transfer of the business from the current Franchisee to a new Franchisee.

Meet the New Authors

With the passing of Erwin Keup, the originator and founding author of *Entrepreneur* magazine's *Franchise Bible* series, the baton has been passed to the new authors to carry on the mission of educating franchise entrepreneurs around the world.

RICHARD GROSSMANN

Mr. Grossmann has been involved in the franchise industry since 1994. He franchised his first company and grew it to 49 franchised locations in 19 states during the mid to late '90s. He served as the CEO and primary trainer focusing on franchisee relations and creating tools and technologies to increase franchisee success.

Rick franchised his second company in 2003. He served as the company's CEO and Marketing Director. He developed the high tech/high touch franchise marketing and sales system, selling over 150 franchises in North America capturing a ranking in *Entrepreneur* magazine's Franchise 500® in less than three years.

During this period Mr. Grossmann also served as a business and marketing consultant to small companies and multimillion-dollar enterprises. He also consulted franchisees and prospective franchisees, franchisors, and companies seeking to become franchisors.

Rick had the honor of working with his mentor, Erwin Keup as a contributing author for this book's seventh edition, published by Entrepreneur Press.

Mr. Grossmann currently serves as the president of My Franchise Hub and Vet Starter in the Greenwood Village area near Denver, Colorado.

MICHAEL J. KATZ ESQ.

Mr. Katz is a practicing attorney in Colorado and is a senior partner and managing member of Corporon & Katz, LLC. Mr. Katz has been practicing law for over 33 years, during which time he has limited his practice to the areas of franchise, real estate, and business law. He represents franchisors and franchisees from around the United States and has clients in Europe and Australia.

He is an active member of the American Bar Association subcommittees on Franchising and Business. Mr. Katz is the recipient of the *Franchise Times* Legal Eagle award that recognizes practitioners that deliver outstanding service to the franchise field. He is also listed by the American Registry as one of the top 1 percent of lawyers nationwide and has the highest rating awarded by Martindale Hubbell. Michael also served as a contributing author for the seventh edition of this book.

INDEX

Note: Page numbers in italics indicate figures; page numbers in bold indicate tables.